THE BALLADS
OF
MARKO KRALJEVIĆ

MARKO AND SHARATZ

THE BALLADS
OF
MARKO KRALJEVIĆ

TRANSLATED BY

D. H. LOW

FORMERLY LECTURER IN ENGLISH
IN THE UNIVERSITY OF BELGRADE

CAMBRIDGE
AT THE UNIVERSITY PRESS
1922

TO

MY WIFE

CAMBRIDGE
UNIVERSITY PRESS

University Printing House, Cambridge CB2 8BS, United Kingdom

Cambridge University Press is part of the University of Cambridge.

It furthers the University's mission by disseminating knowledge in the pursuit of
education, learning and research at the highest international levels of excellence.

www.cambridge.org
Information on this title: www.cambridge.org/9781107505421

First published 1922
First paperback edition 2015

A catalogue record for this publication is available from the British Library

ISBN 978-1-107-50542-1 Paperback

TABLE OF CONTENTS

[vi]

P L A T E

MARKO AND SHARATZ   FRONTISPIECE
[From a drawing by Olive Carleton Smyth]

* These two ballads are obviously inferior to the others. In the 1913 edition they are placed after the "Death of Marko." With this exception the order of that edition has been followed here.

NOTE ON PRONUNCIATION OF PROPER NAMES

In order to avoid some of the difficulties of transliteration the Croatian alphabet has been generally used throughout the book.

š = English sh as in ship

č = „ ch „ chill

ž = French j „ jour

dž = English j „ James

ć = „ ty „ Luttyens

c = „ ts „ rats

j = „ y „ yes

Examples: Šarac; Jabučilo; Samodreža; Kesedžija.

INTRODUCTION

I

IN the seventeenth and eighteenth centuries, before Western Europe suspected the existence of a great traditional folk-poetry among the Southern Slavs, the *literati* of Ragusa had occasionally amused themselves by writing down the songs and ballads current among the people. These manuscript copies were handed round and read within the very small and select circle of the initiate, but remained unknown to the outer world until the middle of the nineteenth century. There was one important exception. This was the work of the Franciscan monk Andrija Kačić Miošić[1], who, in 1756, published in Venice his *Razgovor ugodni naroda slovinskoga*, a book which had immediate success in Dalmatia and the islands. It was not a collection of genuine folk-songs, although the old traditional themes formed the basis of it. Kačić was fired with a missionary zeal for what he conceived to be historical truth, and as he was deeply read in the chronicles of his race, he altered, adapted and supplemented his material accordingly[2]. The result which he aimed at, and which he achieved, was to produce an ordered account of Slavonic kings and heroes in such form as would make the strongest appeal to his fellow-countrymen by stimulating their pride of race. In the whole collection there are only two or three indubitable folk-ballads, and even these have been manipulated in the interest of an illusory truth to fact. Notwithstanding the artifice of the work,

---

[1] Andrija Kačić Miošić (1690–1760) was a native of Makarska in Dalmatia. Generally known as Kačić. The first known edition of the *Razgovor ugodni* appeared in 1756. In 1757 Bodmer printed the *Kriemhilden Rache und die Klage* and, as Carlyle remarks, "a certain antiquarian tendency in literature, a fonder, more earnest looking back into the Past, began about that time to manifest itself in all nations." *The Nibelungen Lied*, p. 1.

[2] *Das serbische Volkslied in der deutschen Literatur*, by Dr Milan Ćurčin, Leipzig, 1905, p. 21.

Kačić made such skilful use of his themes, his additions and alterations were made with such easy mastery of traditional epithet and formula, that the South Slavs themselves overlooked the signs of modern treatment and accepted the book as a genuine record of the past. Numerous manuscript copies were made, certain pieces found their way into the rustic repertory, so that peasants and countrymen sang songs from Kačić in the fields.

Hitherto, the interest in Kačić had been entirely confined to the narrow limits of his own people, and even there, although the songs in the *Razgovor* were remembered and repeated, the name of the maker tended to sink into oblivion. But in 1760, the very year in which Kačić died, there was published in Edinburgh the first instalment of Macpherson's *Ossian*[1]. The effect on the weary literature of the time was magical. Here was something strange and fresh and compelling! A wind from the wide spaces of sea and moorland blew into the crowded haunts of men, and under the new influence the forgotten treasures of ballad poetry were eagerly sought after and as eagerly displayed. The appearance of Percy's *Reliques* marks a turning-point in literary history. It is true that Percy manipulated his material with less adroitness than either Kačić or Macpherson, he nevertheless rescued a number of venerable ballads from impending destruction, the new spirit breathed authentically in him and his book became an inspiration[2].

Immense as was the influence of *Ossian* and the *Reliques* in Britain, it was perhaps even greater in Germany and on the Continent generally. The world was ripe for a breach with a monotonous literary convention. The polished age, the age of good sense, yearned in its heart for the primitive and the passionate. *Ossian* became a fever, an obsession that revealed itself often in childish and extravagant ways. All over Europe rocking-cradles

---

[1] *Fragments of Ancient Poetry collected in the Highlands of Scotland and translated from the Gaelic or Erse Language*, Edinburgh, 1760, 70 pp.

[2] "I do not think there is a writer in verse of the present day who would not be proud to acknowledge his obligation to the *Reliques*." Wordsworth, Appendix to Preface to 2nd ed. of *Lyrical Ballads*.

lulled infant Oscars to sleep, the Royal House of Scandinavia adopted the name as one worthy of its kingly line, and on Goethe's youthful hero the Celtic Muse produced all the symptoms of intoxication. "Homer," cries Werther, "has been superseded in my heart by the divine Ossian. Through what a world does this angelic bard carry me!" The sentiment is, doubtless, a not unfaithful reflection of the poet's own attitude at the time, and he was one of many.

In Italy we can trace the same chain of cause and effect, and it is to an Italian, the Abbate Alberto Fortis, that the credit is due of acting as the first interpreter between the Serbs and the more cultured peoples of the West. A well-known naturalist in his day, he was personally acquainted with Cesarotti the translator of *Ossian*, and was himself a profound admirer of Macpherson's gloomy genius. The importance of this preoccupation is that when he made his expeditions to Dalmatia and the Adriatic islands, his mind was already prepared to observe and note any evidence there might be of the existence of an oral tradition among the people[1]. Being but very imperfectly acquainted with the Serbian language, he was unable to address himself directly to the peasants, and was therefore entirely dependent in this respect on the good offices of his learned Dalmatian friends. These latter supplied him with examples of alleged folk-song and helped in the task of translating them into Italian.

In 1771 Fortis published his *Saggio d' Osservazioni sopra l' isola di Cherso ed Osero*, in which there appeared the first translation from the Serbian into a modern tongue. It was the "Canto di Milos Cobilich e di Vuko Brankovich[2]." The poem as here given comes from Kačić, a fact of which Fortis was evidently ignorant, although how it happened that his Dalmatian friends did not enlighten him is a point that has never been explained. They may have regarded Kačić as a mere compiler of national ballads, and so considered his name as of small

---

[1] Ćurčin, *op. cit.* p. 22.

[2] Miloš Obilić is the hero and Vuk Branković the traitor of the Kossovo cycle.

importance, or they may possibly have committed the piece to writing as it was actually sung by the country-folk, but this is conjecture.

Three years later Fortis published his *Viaggio in Dalmazia*, a work of much greater importance. A complete section of the book is devoted to the manners and customs of the "Morlacks[1]" (De' Costumi de' Morlacchi), and to a chapter on their poetry and music there is appended as an example of the former, the poem afterwards made famous by Goethe under the title of "Klaggesang von der edlen Frauen des Asan Aga."

This ballad was printed by Fortis in the original Serbian together with a parallel translation in Italian, and is presented with the apologetic air common to the early collectors[2]. "I have translated several heroic songs of the Morlacchi," he writes, "and several of them appear to me to be both well-conducted and interesting, but I very readily allow that they cannot be put in comparison with the poems of the celebrated Scotch bard which we have lately had the pleasure of seeing translated into our own language with true poetical spirit by the Abbé Cesarotti[3]."

The source from which the "Klaggesang" was derived remained for long a mystery. It is not in Kačić and only in 1883 when Miklošić published the text of a manuscript sent to him by friends in Ragusa, was the problem at last solved[4]. It is now clear that Fortis must have had this MS. or a close variant of it before him when he made his own copy, and as luck would have it, this particular poem is a perfect specimen of its kind.

In 1775 a translation by Werthes of the Morlacchian section was published at Berne as *Die Sitten der Morlacken*, and next

[1] A name of disputed origin. For Fortis' opinion on the subject, see *Travels into Dalmatia*, pp. 46–47. London, 1778.

[2] Cf. Percy: "In a polished age like the present, I am sensible that many of these reliques of antiquity will require great allowances to be made for them."

[3] *Travels into Dalmatia* (English trans. of the *Viaggio*). London, 1778.

[4] *Über Goethes Klaggesang von der edlen Frauen des Asan Aga.* Vienna, 1883. See Ćurčin, p. 43.

year the same author produced the complete work under the title of *Reise in Dalmazien*[1]. With Teutonic fidelity he reproduced the Serbian text of the "Klaggesang" including misprints —and gave an accurate rendering of Fortis' Italian version. This book, containing the Serbian original and the German translation of the Italian translation, was the material before Goethe when he set to work on that rendering of his own which has taken its place as a little masterpiece of the translator's art.

Although it has been shown that Fortis was first in the field, it must be stated here that the specimens of Serbian folk-song to which he drew the attention of the learned, owed their wider publicity to the efforts of Herder and the happy collaboration of a poet of world-wide renown. Stimulated thereto by the romantic revival in England, Herder had begun his celebrated collections of folk-poetry. He did not confine his labours to the German field, his taste was catholic and he laid under contribution all nations and all tongues. Thus in the first part of the *Volkslieder* (1778) we find two pieces from the Serbian: the first, translated by Herder himself, is entitled "Ein Gesang von Milos Cobilich[2] und Vuko Brankovich, Morlakisch." The other, the "Klaggesang von der edlen Frauen des Asan Aga," is the work of Goethe[3].

In 1779 Herder published the second volume of *Volkslieder*. It contained two additional pieces from the Serbian, namely,

[1] A French translation, *Voyage en Dalmatie—par M. l'Abbé Fortis*, was published at Berne in 1778.

[2] Miloš Obilić or Kobilić. See below, p. xxvi, footnote. He was an intimate friend of Marko's. Vuk Branković was the traitor who is said to have deserted from the Serbs during the course of the struggle at Kossovo.

[3] Sir Walter Scott translated the "Klaggesang" under the title of "Morlachian Fragment—after Goethe." Lockhart seems to suggest that this was printed in the *Apology for Tales of Terror* (1799). Only twelve copies of the *Apology* were printed (cf. Lockhart, vol. i. p. 275. Macmillan, 1900), of which one is now in the library at Abbotsford. On inspecting this copy, however, I found no trace of the "Morlachian Fragment." On the flyleaf Scott has written: "This was the first book printed by Ballantyne of Kelso—only twelve copies were thrown off and none for sale." The book contains 79 pages and the Table of Contents is as follows:

1. The Erl-King.
2. The Water-King. A Danish ballad.

"Radoslaus. Eine Morlakische Geschichte," and "Die schöne Dolmetscherin. Eine Morlakische Geschichte." These four ballads derived one and all from Fortis, but it was their appearance in Herder's collection that definitely marks the introduction of Serbian literature to the reading public of the West. No great development, however, took place until Vuk Stefanović Karadžić began his monumental labours in Vienna[1]. With the unfailing encouragement and support of the Slovene scholar Jernej Kopitar, Vuk completed in the course of his long life an almost incredible amount of work of first-rate importance. It was in 1813 that Kopitar showed him Goethe's translation. The following year Vuk published his *Kleine Serbische Grammatik*, and the first modest instalment of his unrivalled collections of Serbian folk-song. In 1815 he made the acquaintance of Jacob Grimm who had come to Vienna as a delegate to the International Congress then sitting. The possibilities of the work in which Vuk was engaged immediately arrested his attention. The translations in the *Volkslieder* whilst indicating the quality of Serbian song had given no hint of the quantitative aspect, and Grimm was filled with astonishment at the unsuspected richness of the hoard which Vuk was then revealing to the world. He addressed himself at once to the study of the language, and his zeal increased with his knowledge. Goethe's interest in the *Volkslied* faded, flickered up again and failed, but Grimm remained true to his first conviction that the most significant literary event of his time was the discovery of the traditional poetry of the Serbs. He himself translated a number of Vuk's pieces, and in articles, reviews and prefaces insisted on the unique value of the Serbian minstrelsy. More than any other of foreign birth he contributed to place the study of this literature on a sound and solid basis.

3. Lord William.
4. Poor Mary—The Maid of the Inn. By Mr Southey.
5. The Chase.
6. William and Helen.
7. Monzo the Brave and Fair Imogine.
8. Arthur and Matilda.
9. The Erl-King's Daughter.

[1] Vuk Stefanović Karadžić (1787–1864). See Appendix, p. 180 ff.

In 1818 the first edition of Vuk's *Dictionary* appeared, which in its later form became an encyclopaedia of information and remains to this day an indispensable work of reference. The same year saw the publication in Berlin of Förster's *Sängerfahrt*, of interest here as it contained nineteen Serbian songs[1] translated by Jacob Grimm. Grimm held very definite opinions on the manner in which such renderings should be made. In his view there were two alternatives: either an almost word for word prose translation, or a version of the sort that was possible only to a Goethe[2].

The cult of the Serbian folk-song in Germany did not fail to attract attention in France. Madame de Staël hastened to assure Goethe that she was "ravie de la femme morlaque." In 1788 Justine Wynne published *Les Morlaques*, a book based on the work of Fortis[3]. Charles Nodier followed in 1821 with his *Smarra*, purporting to be a collection of Slavonic songs and tales. These, like the songs in *Les Morlaques*, were largely spurious; nevertheless, they served a certain purpose—as did Mérimée's literary jest, *La Guzla*—in preparing the way for honest and serious work such as Dozon's *Poésies populaires serbes* (1859).

[1] The first of these is "Marko's Hunting with the Turks." Grimm's title is "Die Jagd Muleys"; cf. Ćurčin, p. 103, footnote; Grimm's *Kleinere Schriften*, iv. pp. 455–458. This is the only Marko ballad given by Grimm.

[2] Nevertheless Grimm made translations in verse as well as in prose. The pieces in the *Sängerfahrt* are non-metrical, line by line translations keeping extraordinarily closely to the original, but a number of renderings in the appropriate measures will be found collected in the *Kl. Schr.* iv. pp. 427–455.

[3] *Les Morlaques, par J.W.C.D.U. et R.* (Justine Wynne, Comtesse de Ursins-Rosenberg). Venice, 1788. Writing in 1825 Goethe says: "Schon sind es fünfzig Jahre, dass ich den Klaggesang der edlen Frauen Asan Agas übersetzte, der sich in des Abbate Fortis Reise, auch von da in den Morlackischen Notizen der Gräfin Rosenberg finden liess. Ich übertrug ihn nach dem beigefügten Französischen, mit Ahnung des Rhythmus und Beachtung der Wortstellung des Originals." Essay on "Serbische Lieder" in *Über Kunst und Alterthum*, 5 Band, 2 Heft, p. 35. (In Hempel's edition of *Goethe's Works*, vol. 29, p. 583.) Ćurčin, pp. 47–51. Ćurčin shows conclusively that Goethe suffered from a *lapsus memoriae* in making the statement above quoted.

To return to the main stream of German endeavour, we find a woman, Fräulein von Jacob, taking the lead in the task of translation. Her full name was Therese Albertine Luise von Jacob, whence she derived her somewhat awkward pseudonym of Talvj. Introduced by Grimm to the work of Vuk, and learning that her idol Goethe was interested in the subject, she was carried away by an eager desire to do something that would attract his attention to herself. Forthwith she plunged impetuously into correspondence with the veteran poet, and her hopes were not disappointed, for Goethe proved not unwilling to play the part of benevolent counsellor and friend to a young and charming lady of literary talent. Thus encouraged Talvj went enthusiastically to work. In 1825 the first volume of her *Volkslieder der Serben* appeared, and was followed by the second volume the year after. It is an important book, for although Talvj lacked poetical insight and worked at a speed incompatible with a fastidious choice of words, she was the first to present to the German public, and so to the world at large, a copious and systematic selection of the rich material collected and printed by Vuk[1].

Her work was well received and was fruitful in many directions. One particular result deserves special notice, for it was the publication of the *Volkslieder der Serben* that prompted Sir John Bowring to produce his *Servian Popular Poetry*[2] (1827), the first attempt to introduce the subject to English readers. The dedication, in verse, is addressed to "Dr Steph. Vuk Karadjich." It is uncommonly bad verse. Fortunately it is by far the worst thing in the book. The introduction is instructive, but in the course of it the author makes the curious mistake of referring to the gusle as a "three-stringed instrument." "The historical ballads," he continues, "which are in lines composed of five trochaics, are always sung with the accompaniment of the Gusle. At the end of every verse the singer drops his voice and mutters

---

[1] Народне Српске Пјесме—*Servian Popular Poetry*, translated by John Bowring. London, 1827. It should be noted that a book entitled "Translations from the Servian Minstrelsy" was printed for private circulation in 1826. See *Quarterly Review* in Bibliography.
[2] Cf. Grimm, *Kl. Schr.* IV. pp. 419–421.

a short cadence. The emphatic passages are chanted in a louder tone. 'I cannot describe,' says Wessely, 'the pathos with which these songs are sometimes sung. I have witnessed crowds surrounding a blind old singer and every cheek was wet with tears—it was not the music, it was the words that affected them.'" (Introduction, p. xliv.)

With regard to his predecessors Bowring remarks: "The translations which have appeared in Germany under the name of Talvj, are the work of an amiable woman (Theresa von Jacob) who, having passed the earlier part of her life in Russia, and possessing a mind cultivated by literature and captivated by the natural beauties of Servian poetry, has most successfully devoted herself to their diffusion. Professor Eugenius Wessely, of Vinkovcze in Slavonia, has also published a small volume of Translations from the Nuptial Songs of the Servians[1]. The renderings have the merit of perfect fidelity, and his introduction contains many interesting illustrations of Servian manners....To fidelity at least, this volume may lay an honest claim. I have endeavoured to avail myself of all the authors who have written on the subject, particularly of the valuable criticisms of Dr Kopitar in the Vienna *Jahrbuch der Literatur*, of the works of Goethe, Grimm and Vater. The notes attached to Talvj's translation I have employed without any special reference to them."

On comparing the *Servian Popular Poetry* with her own *Volkslieder der Serben*, Talvj came to the conclusion that Bowring was indebted to her for more than the notes, and the lady cherished a certain resentment against the author for concealing, as she thought, the extent of his indebtedness. He had a certain fluent and agreeable knack, which, although it urged him sometimes to the verge of the namby-pamby, is employed, upon the whole, effectively enough. It would be unjust as well as ungenerous to decry the work of Bowring, but it is the date of his book and the complete absence of rival translations which give

[1] E. Eugen Wesely was a gymnasium professor at Vinkovce. His book containing metrical translations of fifty wedding-songs from Vuk's collection was published at Pest in 1826. Cf. Grimm, *Kl. Schr.* iv. p. 421.

him a place apart[1]. A whole generation elapsed before another Englishman came to glean in the same rich field.

In 1828 Wilhelm Gerhard published at Leipzig his *Wila: Serbische Volkslieder und Heldenmärchen*. His work included a good deal of material from Vuk untranslated by Talvj, and contained also pieces not given by Vuk but communicated by Gerhard's friend Milutinović, together with a selection from Kačić. To the second volume was attached a bulky "Appendix," consisting of a translation of Mérimée's *Guzla*, for he was one of those who were completely deceived by the Frenchman's *tour de force*[2]. Gerhard alone was responsible for the unfortunate blunder. The rest of the book, which was the joint work of Gerhard and Milutinović, may be regarded as a satisfactory amplification of the translations of Talvj.

It must strike the reader of this sketch as remarkable that hitherto the name of no Austrian translator has been mentioned. Vuk, the great mainspring of the movement, had his home in Vienna; moreover the Austrian capital for geographical and political reasons was in much closer touch with the Southern Slavs than any other city in Europe, yet characteristically enough Austrian savants and men of letters neglected the opportunity, and so for many years it was left to their more purposeful and energetic fellow-Teutons in Germany to exploit the field. At last, however, Austria bestirred herself. In 1850, Anastasius Grün published a number of translations from the Slovene under the title of *Volkslieder aus Krain*. Frankl followed with his *Gusle, Serbische Nationallieder*, dedicated to Vuk's daughter. His object was to present some of the songs in Vuk which had not yet been translated, and he took the greatest pains to reproduce in German the metrical effect of the Serbian originals. A very interesting development now took place. The earliest collectors, from Kačić onwards, had shown a marked and natural disposition

[1] Only three of the Marko ballads are given by Bowring. They are: "The Moorish King's Daughter," "Marko and the Turks," and the "Death of Kralevich Marko." See pp. 104, 146, 174 of this translation.

[2] In the preface to the 2nd edition of *La Guzla*, Mérimée says that two months after the publication of the book Bowring wrote to him with a request for copies of the originals.

to group the heroic songs together so as to form, if possible, some
sort of coherent sequence. Vuk had already attempted to arrange
the Marko ballads[1]. Vogl made a more ambitious effort in the
same direction, supplementing Vuk's material with other Marko
songs from Milutinović, and the method was pushed to its logical
conclusion by Kapper who, in his *Lazar der Serbencar*, knit
together the ballads of the Kossovo cycle and produced therefrom
a single complete poem[2].

Before our eyes, as it were, we have a demonstration of the
genesis of an epic. It is true that Kapper's *Lazar* is an artificial
product. The conditions essential to the birth, or rebirth, of
the epic were passing rapidly away, but it is as certain as such
things can be that if the Turkish dominion had endured a
century or two longer, the separate ballads of the Kossovo cycle
chanted by the Serbian guslari would have fused together as
did the Nibelungen songs of the Germanic Spielleute[3].

In 1859 the French consul at Belgrade published a remarkable
book entitled *Poésies populaires serbes*, consisting of a line-by-line
non-metrical rendering of five Kossovo songs, twelve Marko
ballads in prose[4], a number of Hajduk pieces, a selection of seven
heroic poems and some of the so-called "domestic" or "family"

[1] A very difficult task. See below, note 3.
[2] Kapper had a Serbian predecessor in the person of Joxim Nović-
Otoćanin who published his *Lazarica* at Novi Sad (Neusatz) in 1847.
The name "Lazarica" has since been generally adopted to denote
the Kossovo cycle.
[3] In the Kossovo cycle there is a definite chronological sequence of
events highly favourable to the ultimate union of the fragments into
a coherent whole.
The Marko ballads, on the other hand, resist such treatment. It is
difficult to establish any satisfactory progression in time and equally
difficult to arrange the stories so as to trace any development in Marko's
character. It may be that the epic ballads as we have them now are
merely recast fragments of longer epic poems now lost. If so then
the modern attempts to join up these fragments are in the nature of
a reversal of the process of disintegration.
[4] 1. Ouroch et les Merniavtchévitch.
   2. Marko et la Vila.
   3. Marko et le faucon.
   4. Les noces de Marko.

songs, including "The Wife of Hassan Aga." It is an admirable
work. The introduction, the notes and the translations are sound
and reliable, and as an introduction to the subject, it is the most
generally useful book that has appeared since Talvj.

Two years later, we find in Owen Meredith's *Serbski Pesme,
National Songs of Servia*, another attempt to interpret Serbian
folk-song to Englishmen[1]. Regarded as poetry, these versions are
on a much higher level than Bowring's, but the author allowed
himself much greater liberty of treatment. As he says himself,
"no attempt has been made at accurate verbal translation from
the original language. They cannot, indeed, be called translations
in the strict sense of the word. What they are, let the reader
decide." The first seventy-five pages are devoted to a spirited
rendering of the Kossovo ballads and the second half of the book
consists of "Popular or Domestic Pesmas" among which is to
be found once more "The Wife of Hassan Aga[2]."

The wide attention that had been given to Serbian literature
was part of the universal romantic movement. But it was no
longer new. Foreign interest had reached its high-water mark
and was now failing rapidly. Writing in 1905, Dr Ćurčin de-
plored the fact that Germans knew less about Serbian literature

5. Marko reconnaît le sabre de son père.
6. Marko et le bey Kostadin.
7. Marko et Alil-Aga.
8. Marko et la fille du roi des Maures.
9. Marko va à la chasse avec les Turcs.
10. Marko laboureur.
11. Mort de Marko.
12. La sœur du Capitaine Léka (Analyse).

[1] Owen Meredith, the pen-name of Edward Robert, first Earl of
Lytton (1831–1892). He was Viceroy of India in 1876 and was
Ambassador in Paris at the time of his death.

[2] Owen Meredith in his Introduction acknowledges his indebtedness
to Dozon's work, and indeed certain passages are transferred almost
literally from the French, *e.g.* "Il (Marko) est de la famille des Roland,
des Cid, des Roustem (et aussi des Gargantua)," Dozon, Introd.
p. 20; "féroce comme un Viking scandinave," p. 13. "Marko Kralie-
vitch...a sort of burly, brawling Viking of the land, with just a touch
in his composition of Roland and the Cid, but with much more about
him of Gargantua," Introd. p. xxvii, Owen Meredith.

then than they did half a century before. Since then, however,
the political destiny of the Serbs has brought home to the world
the great qualities of these people, their unswerving loyalty to
their friends, their indomitable courage in disaster, their
moderation in the hour of victory.

By its own intrinsic excellence the Serbian folk-poetry takes
a very high place indeed, but there is another reason in a different
order of ideas why the ballads should be read and studied. All
the members of the Serbian race, so long politically held apart,
are now united in the new Kingdom of the Serbs, Croats and
Slovenes. The rivalries of the component parts are certainly
bitter; the forces of disintegration are powerful and even
dangerous but the Serbian race has become the Serbian nation, a
gifted and imaginative nation with a future of brilliant promise
before it. To understand this people, to grasp the circumstances
that have shaped their mentality, has become a matter of practical
importance, and to this end there is no surer guide than the
national poetry: it leads straight to the people's heart. "You may
still find many an illiterate person in Serbia, but you will not
find one who would not be able to tell you something about
Stephan Nemanya, the first king of mediaeval Serbia, about his
son St Sava, Tsar Doushan, his young son Ourosh, King
Voukashin, the Royal Prince Kralyevitch Marko, Tsar Lazar,
and the heroes who fell in the famous battle at Kossovo[1]." That
is truly said, and of all the old traditional heroes Marko is the
best-beloved. There is no key to the soul of Serbia like a wise
and sympathetic study of the ballads of Marko Kraljević.

[1] Chedo Mijatovich in preface to *Hero-tales and Legends of the
Serbians*, by W. M. Petrovitch. London, 1914.

MARKO KRALJEVIĆ

H ISTORY has very little to say concerning Marko. The facts can be stated in a few words. He was the son of Vukašin, King of Prilep, hence the appellation Kraljević, or King's son, by which he is universally known.

In 1371, Vukašin and his brother Uglješ, as members of a very loose species of Balkan League, made an attempt to repel the Turkish invaders. But the Turks surprised and routed the Serbian army at Tchermen on the Marica, and Vukašin was drowned in the river along with thousands of his men[1]. Marko succeeded his father as King of Prilep but the Ottoman pressure was irresistible, and in order, presumably, to retain his lands and local authority, Marko went over to the service of the Turk (1385). One of the Serbian MSS. in the Khludov collection at Moscow says that Marko was married in this town to Helen, daughter of the Vojvod Chlapen. There is no record of his having been present at the battle of Kossovo, although it is probable that he did play some part in the struggle. He was killed, according to tradition, at the battle of Rovina in 1394, while fighting for the army of the Sultan Bajazet against the Roumanians[2].

That is practically all the information we have and there is no body or substance in it. Yet every Serb knows and loves Marko, and reveres him as the greatest hero of the race. It is the traditional poetry that has wrought this marvel, that has atoned for the silence of history, that has endowed Kraljević with a robust vitality. Without it the great Marko would have been but the shadow of a shade.

Before dealing with the epic ballads wherein the exploits of

[1] See *History of Serbia* by H. W. V. Temperley (London, 1917), p. 95. Also Dozon, *op. cit.* p. 70 f.

[2] Vuk's *Rječnik*, under art. "Marko Kraljević." See translation in appendix. Also Temperley, pp. 97–98. In the ballads there is certainly an attempt to establish a connection between Marko and Kossovo but it is very perfunctory. See "Marko and the Falcon."

the Serbian Hercules are recorded, let us look for a little at the
historical picture of his time. He lived at one of the great turning-
points of history: the period of the Turkish irruption into Europe.
It is a confused and confusing period, through the tangled mazes
of which Gibbon is still the best guide.

In 1354, Suleiman, a son of the Emir Orkhan, occupied
Gallipoli, the key of the Hellespont, and the forward sweep of
Ottoman conquest had begun. The following year, Tsar Stepan
Dushan, the maker and the Emperor of Great Serbia, left
Prizren his capital and moved eastwards. It was his wish to be
recognised as the champion of Christendom. Unfortunately he
had failed to obtain either the whole-hearted support of the Pope
at Avignon or the assistance of the Venetian fleet[1]. He had just
concluded a severe struggle with the King of Hungary and his
Magyars, by whom he had been wantonly attacked. None the
less, having reorganised his forces, he now pressed forward
against the Turk with reasonable prospect of success. It is quite
clear that, better than any of his contemporaries, he had grasped
the significance of the advent of the invaders, and it was his
present purpose to thrust them back into Asia, seize Constantinople from the hands of the effete Cantacuzenus and convert
the city into the seat of government of a huge consolidated
Slavonic Empire. Dushan was one of the great captains of his
age, his plans were boldly yet carefully conceived, but when
almost within sight of the goal the Serbian Emperor died a
mysterious death[2]. The succession passed to his young son Urosh,
who proved utterly unable to control the disruptive elements in
the State, and the imposing edifice reared by the father began
to crumble to pieces under the son. The house was divided against
itself and its fall was only a matter of time. Released from the
compelling power of a master-spirit, the Serbs split up into

[1] Temperley, pp. 76–77. Jireček's account gives the impression
that Dushan's chances of success against Constantinople had been almost
fatally compromised by the attack made upon him by King Lewis
and his Hungarians.

[2] Jireček, *Geschichte der Serben*, pp. 407–412; the place of Dushan's
death is unknown. Ranke, *History of Servia* (Bohn, 1853), p. 15;
Temperley, *History of Serbia*, pp. 76–78.

factions under Vukašin, Lazar and others, and the crowd of
vassal potentates, refusing allegiance to Urosh, strove each to
establish complete independence within his own domain[1].

It is quite possible, as Freeman thought, that if Tsar Dushan
had lived to seize Constantinople, a bulwark would have been
raised capable of withstanding the Turks: "Servia would have
been the body and Constantinople the head. As it was the Turks
found in Servia a body without a head, and in Constantinople
a head without a body[2]."

In 1359, four years after Tsar Dushan's untimely death, the
warlike Suleiman was thrown from his horse and killed, but his
brother, Sultan Murad I, carried on with resistless energy the
policy of aggression. "By the pale and fainting light of the
Byzantine annals," says Gibbon, "we can discern that he sub-
dued without resistance the whole province of Romania or
Thrace from the Hellespont to Mount Haemus and the verge
of the capital, and that Adrianople was chosen for the royal seat
of his government in Europe." Adrianople fell to Murad in
1361, Philippopoli in 1363. In 1371 he overthrew Vukašin in
the battle on the Maritza—the ancient Hebrus—and in 1375
he took Nish (Nissa), the birthplace of Constantine[3]. Events were
now moving to a crisis. The capture of Nish gave the Turks a
position of such military advantage that unless they could be
ejected it was certain that the invaders would ultimately reduce
the Balkans to servitude. Once more the dire need of some sort
of united action seems to have penetrated the Slav consciousness,
and roused the chiefs to at least a partial realisation of the ex-
tremity of their common peril. It was now that the Lord of
North Serbia, Knez Lazar (the Tsar Lazar of the ballads), made

[1] Cf. "Uroš and the Mrnjavčevići" and "The Death of Dushan"
in this translation. Uroš was 19 years of age at the time of his succession.
He was "a youth of great parts, quiet and gracious, but without experience." This is the description of contemporary Serbian chroniclers
quoted by Prof. Tihomir R. Djordjević in *The Battle of Kossovo*,
p. 11, published by the Kossovo Day Committee, 1917.

[2] Freeman, *The Ottoman Power in Europe* (Macmillan, 1877), p. 106.

[3] The date of the permanent Turkish occupation of Nish is uncertain.
Prof. Djordjević puts it as late as 1386. Cf. Temperley, p. 99, footnote.

a supreme effort to stem the advancing tide. In alliance with
Tvrtko, King of Bosnia, he won a victory over the Turks on
Toplitza river in 1387. Encouraged by this success, the Bulgarians
who had already been compelled to submit to Turkish over-lord-
ship, threw off their allegiance, but in the course of the following
year Amurath[1] succeeded in crushing them once more, and
turned about to deal with the Serbian foe. In the meantime the
Serbs had rallied to Lazar's standard at Krushevatz, and on the
28th of June (O.S. June 15th), 1389, "Tsar" and Sultan met
in bloody strife on the sun-parched plain of Kossovo. "In the
battle of Kossovo," writes Gibbon, "the league and independence
of the Sclavonian tribes was finally crushed[2]. As the conqueror
walked over the field, he observed that the greatest part of the
slain consisted of beardless youths, and listened to the flattering
reply of the vizier that age and wisdom would have taught them
not to oppose his irresistible arms. But the sword of his janizaries
could not save him from the dagger of despair: a Serbian soldier
started from the crowd of dead bodies, and Amurath was pierced
in the belly with a mortal wound." The struggle thus briefly
described by the great historian was one of the decisive battles
of the world. The South Slav barrier had broken down, and thereafter the Turkish storm-wave was destined to surge forward across
Europe to break furiously at last against the walls of Vienna.

[1] This name occurs as "Amurath," "Murad" and "Murat."

[2] "Historically," says Sir Arthur Evans, "the battle of Kossovo was
essentially a drawn battle....It was not without reason that the com-
mander of the Bosnian and Primorian contingent, Vlatko Hranitch,
who drew off his own forces from the field in good order, sent tidings
of victory to his master, King Tvrtko, passed on by him to the citizens
of Traü and Florence. In the Cathedral of Notre Dame, *Te Deums*
of thanksgiving for the success of the Christian arms were actually
celebrated in the presence of the King of France....Thus the first
impression of the fight was that of an heroic combat between equals.
*The bards who carried on the Court poetry that had already existed in
the days of Tsar Dushan and earlier kings, dramatized the incidents of
the battle without any particular reference to historic consequences.* It was
only the later realization of its far-reaching effects that made the Lay
of Kossovo an epic record of what proved to have been the last united
effort of the Serbian race to resist the Asiatic invader." *Serbia's Greatest
Battle*, published by the Kossovo Day Committee, 1917.

L. S. B.   c

The heroic memory of Kossovo, for all its aftermath of ruin and despair, wrought fruitfully in the Serbian soul in the form of the celebrated ballad-cycle now known as the "Lazarica," which after an age-long existence in the form of oral tradition was set down in writing in the first half of last century. The doughty deeds there recorded are described naturally with a view to the glorification of the vanquished. Gibbon's nameless soldier is none other than Milosh Obilitch who penetrated, under vow, to the Sultan's tent and slew him there[1]. But the death of the Sultan in no way affected the issue of the battle. Led by his son Bajazet surnamed Yilderim, the Thunderbolt, the same who afterwards threatened to feed his horse on the high altar of St Peter's at Rome, the Turks shattered the Serb confederation and the hope of a strong united Serbian Empire melted away. Covered with wounds, so the ballad runs, the Tsar's faithful body-servant Milutin spurred his steed from the stricken field and bore the dark tidings to the White Tower of Krushevatz where Lazar's wife Militza sat watching and waiting.

Lazar is dead, he says, and

> Milosh fell,
> Pursued by myriads down the dell,
> Upon Sitnitza's rushy brink,
> Whose chilly waves will roll I think
> So long as time itself doth roll,
> Red with remorse that they roll o'er him.
> Christ have mercy on his soul,
> And blessed be the womb that bore him[2].

[1] Cf. Richard Knolles, *Generall Historie of the Turkes*, p. 200 (ed. 1620): "The name of this man (for his courage worthy of eternal memory) was Miles Cobelitz." The name "Obelić" was, and is, believed by many to be a mere variant of "Kobelić," *i.e.* "Son of a mare." This is what gives point to the jibe of Leka's sister. An example of something of the same sort is to be found in the name Macleod. H. A. Gibbons in his *Ottoman Empire*, p. 177, says: "It is a commentary on the Serbian character that this questionable act has been held up to posterity as the most saintly and heroic deed of national history." Quoted in Temperley's *History of Serbia*, p. 101. Mr Temperley has no difficulty in demolishing the argument.

[2] Owen Meredith, *Serbski Pesme* (reprint, Chatto and Windus, 1917), p. 73.

The dead heroes will live in the memory of Serbs as long as
a man is left and as long as Kossovo plain endures. But as for
Vuk Brankovitch the traitor:

> When the worm and mole
> Are at work on his bones, may his soul
> Eternally singe in Hell-fire.
> Curst be the womb that bore him,
> Curst be his father before him,
> Curst be the race and the name of him
> And foul as his sin be the fame of him,
> For blacker traitor never drew sword,
> False to his faith, to his land, to his lord[1].

Murad's body was interred at Brussa, Lazar's at the monastery
of the New Ravanitsa at Vrdnik in Syrmia[2], but Milosh Obilitch
was buried where he fell. Vuk Brankovitch the traitor, who
deserted with twelve thousand men, survived the battle and
received recompense from the Turks, and when he died they
buried him at Krushevatz, Tsar Lazar's former capital. At the
beginning of last century the Serbian patriots dug up the accurséd
bones and scattered the dishonoured dust to the four winds of
heaven.

[1] Owen Meredith, *op. cit.* p. 75.

[2] To be accurate Lazar's body was at first taken to the monastery
of Gračanica on Kossovo polje. Thence it was removed to the monastery of Ravanica from which place, during the great Serbian exodus,
it was transferred across the Sava to the monastery at Vrdnik in the
Fruška Gora. The monastery was then renamed "Nova Ravanica."

III

THE MARKO OF THE BALLADS

IN the Marko of the ballads we shall look in vain for any attempt on the part of the makers to relate their hero to any of the great historical happenings of the time[1]. Marko is all that matters and his adventures are described with the object of elucidating his character and personality.

The story of King Vukašin's wooing gives a lurid picture of the social conditions of the period, its cruelty, its courage, its unflinching loyalty to blood. Even without the Guslar's statement that Marko followed in his uncle's footsteps, we should have known that the child of such stormy passions was himself predestined to a stormy career. As he grew up Marko developed a strong individuality of his own, and we find Vukašin protesting to the dying Dušan that he has no control over his son. Marko, it appears, drinks and brawls and follows his own wayward course, asking leave of none. Physically he dominates his fellows and his terrifying appearance when in full fighting kit is described in detail again and again. His "Samur kalpak" is pulled low over his dark eyes; his huge black moustache is as large as a lamb of six months' growth; his cloak is a shaggy wolf-pelt; at his girdle swings a damascened blade; on his back is slung a war-spear; at his saddle-bow hangs a mighty mace, with a well-filled wine-skin to hold the balance lest the saddle should slip this way or that.

The steed he bestrides is a wonder-horse[2], the piebald Šarac, his inseparable companion and friend.

---

[1] Vidovit: the word is associated with the idea of second-sight. A child born with a caul is "vidovit"—it knows more than other children and may safely associate with Vilas (Vuk's *Dict.*).

[2] Cf. Chadwick, *The Heroic Age*, p. 440 f.: "On the whole warfare is the state of affairs most commonly involved in heroic stories. It is

When Marko drinks he gives Šarac an equal share of the wine
—"pola pije, pola Šarcu daje[1]"—and the startled observer cries
truthfully that this knight is not as other knights nor this horse
as other horses.

All things considered Marko's character is a surprisingly good
one. He has his evil moments, and he does certain deeds which
cannot be commended, but these are few in number and are not
to be measured against his predominating honesty of purpose, his
self-sacrificing loyalty and the fundamental goodness of his nature.
Let us look for a little at these unworthy deeds of his and consider
their implication. His treatment of Leka's sister appears at first
sight to be horrible and revolting to the last degree[2]. It might be
the act of a Sir Breuse Saunce Pité. Yet when we remember
what the status of woman was, it is evident that in the prelimin-
aries Marko had made Leka an offer which was more than
generous. The damsel had been given the unique privilege of
choosing as her husband one of the three most famous warriors
of the day. How does she respond to this signal mark of honour?
She heaps scorn and insult on the three heroes. Relja she calls
a bastard, Obilić a mare's son, and Marko she flouts as a Turkish
spy. The situation is impossible, beyond belief intolerable, and
a tragic outcome is inevitable. It is the detail of the execution
that shocks the modern mind. But although on broad lines
we may allow Marko to plead justification in this particular case,
what are we to say of his dealings with the daughter of the

a fact worth noting, however, that this warfare almost invariably takes
the form of hand-to-hand fighting and very frequently that of a series
of single combats. *The national aspect of war is seldom brought into
much prominence.*"

   [1] "Marko Kraljević and General Vuča," p. 49, l. 108.
   [2] "The Sister of Leka Kapetan," pp. 29–45, ll. 530–548. It is
interesting to note in this connection that Talvj thoroughly disapproved
of Marko. Goethe also thought him a somewhat rough hero—"ein
rohes Gegenbild zu dem griechischen Herkules, dem persischen Rustan,
aber freilich in scythisch höchst barbarischer Weise." This was the
unfortunate impression gained by a reading of "Marko and the Daughter
of the Moorish King" (p. 104). Later he modified his opinion and
wrote to Talvj asking her to omit from her collection the ballad of
"The Perilous Bogdan." Cf. note, p. 26.

Moorish King[1]? Taken prisoner by the Moors, Marko had languished in a dungeon for seven years, and would have perished there had not the King's daughter offered to set him free on condition that he would swear to be her man. In order to regain his liberty without binding himself to her in any way, Marko employs a puerile device. Squatting in the darkness of the dungeon, he places his cap upon his knees and in solemn accents pledges his word to remain ever faithful—to the cap[2]. The King's daughter, listening at the window, believes naturally that Marko has made oath of fidelity to her. Forthwith she fulfils her part of the bargain, and sets the prisoner free. They ride off together and escape from the country of the Moors. Then comes the tragedy. One morning the dusky beauty approaches Marko with a smile and seeks to embrace him, but a sudden loathing of her swarthy skin overmasters him, he draws his sword and cuts off her head. One other incident may be adduced in illustration of the less admirable side of Marko's nature. On presenting himself at the abode of Philip the Magyar, he is grossly insulted by Philip's wife, and on the spur of the moment he deals her a buffet with his open hand which knocks out "three sound teeth." Assuredly an ungallant deed, but the lady had a vitriolic tongue, and as Marko had taken the trouble to address her with punctilious politeness, her reply causes him to lose his temper. Of the three incidents above mentioned, the killing of the Moorish princess is morally by far the worst. Yet Marko's contemporaries would have thought nothing of such a crime or would have gloried in it as a success gained at the expense of the foe. For by the existing code that deed was virtuous which did scathe to the enemy, to his children or to his children's children. The view that Marko was guilty of treachery in the deceit he practised on the Moorish damsel is out of place here. It was impossible to be treacherous to an enemy; on the other hand it was possible to be generous, and as generosity was such an important part of Marko's make-up, we are disappointed when he falls short in this respect and plays the part of the commonplace ruthless warrior.

[1] P. 104 ff. "Marko and the Daughter of the Moorish King."
[2] Cf. the words of La Flèche, *L'Avare*, Act 1, Sc. 3.

Yet in the event he again reveals his better self, for in his heart he cannot justify the act by reference to a prevailing code, and the redeeming feature is that he suffers bitter remorse, confesses he has done evil and strives by good works to atone for his crime.

The worst that can be said of Marko has now been said. Although Vukašin lamented his wilfulness[1], one of Marko's outstanding characteristics is filial devotion. When his father pursues him with murderous intent, the hero flees from before him because he holds that it were unseemly for son to contend with father[2], and, at a later date, when by chance he meets the Turk who slew Vukašin at the Marica river, Marko exacts fitting vengeance. It is in his relations with his mother, however, that his dutifulness as a son is most strikingly apparent. For her he cherishes an unbounded reverence and love. He constantly seeks her advice and follows it even when it runs counter to all his own natural instincts and desires[3].

His transparent honesty and high moral courage are conspicuous in the fine poem of Uroš and the Mrnjavčevići, when he brushes temptation aside, and, unmindful of consequences to himself, speaks out the truth that is in him.

Essential simplicity and goodness of heart are equally apparent when he rebukes Beg Kostadin for snobbery and unfilial conduct, and upholds the cause of the poor and the unfortunate[4]. Like Robin Hood, with whom he has many points of resemblance, he is ever the friend of the poor and the champion of the oppressed. When the Sultan offers him the post of tax-gatherer with the assurance that great wealth is thus to be obtained, Marko declines the offer on the ground that the poor would curse him[5]. He rescues the distressed damsel from the twelve Moors, and after plying his sabre to such purpose that "of twelve Moors he made twenty-four," he escorts her safely to his own manor where he

---

[1] "The Death of Dushan," p. 10, ll. 43–50.
[2] "Uroš and the Mrnjavčevići," pp. 13–20, ll. 212–218.
[3] *E.g.* "Marko and Djemo the Mountaineer," "The Turks come to Marko's Slava." But in "Marko's Ploughing" he obeys his mother in a humorous way of his own.
[4] "Marko and Beg Kostadin," p. 84.
[5] "Marko and Mina of Kostura," pp. 91–100, ll. 207–232.

gives her into his mother's keeping with strict injunctions that
she is to be treated as if she were his own sister[1].

Ever and always he is eager to redress wrong. A black Moor
from beyond the seas has installed himself as tyrant of Kossovo.
He imposes a wedding-tax on the people and perpetrates shameful
outrage on maid and wife. One day as Marko is passing by, a
maiden of Kossovo laments that she is unable to marry because
her brothers are poor and cannot pay the tax. Marko comforts her
by giving her the necessary sum, gallops off on Šarac to the pavilion
of the oppressor, penetrates within, kills the ruffian and his
attendant satellites and so brings to an abrupt end the outrageous
tyranny beneath which the country groaned. "And all the people,
both great and small, cried: 'God keep Kraljević Marko[2].'"

In a country where lavish hospitality is the rule, Marko's
hospitality has a distinguishing note of its own. During the
celebration of the Slava at Prilep, one of the guests remarks
casually that the feast is perfect save for the lack of fish from
Ochrida. Touched to the quick in his pride as host, Marko
leaves the banquet, saddles Šarac and is about to start for Ochrida
when his mother comes to him and begs him to take no weapons
lest he should shed blood on his Slava day. By a mighty effort of
self-repression, the dutiful son, laying aside his weapons, sets
out unarmed, and on the way meets with the adventure which
proves him to possess in the highest degree the spirit of self-
sacrifice; he is ready to lay down his life for his friends[3].

Another aspect of his nature which must be mentioned here
is his kindly treatment of the lower animals. In the ballad of the
falcon that gave him water to drink and with outspread wings
shielded his head from the glare of the sun, we have a story worthy
of Aesop. Marko in his hour of need is comforted by the humble
creature he had once befriended[4].

Although the times did not encourage the development of
what we should call the sporting instinct, Marko was something

[1] "Marko and the Twelve Moors," pp. 101–103.
[2] "Marko abolishes the Marriage-Tax," p. 139, ll. 247–251.
[3] "Marko and Djemo the Mountaineer," pp. 133–138.
[4] "Marko and the Falcon," p. 58; cf. also variant, p. 59, and
"Marko's Hunting with the Turks," p. 146, ll. 45–46.

of a sportsman. When the crafty damsel outwitted him and made him feel particularly foolish, Marko, after a moment of pardonable fury, bursts into a loud laugh at his own discomfiture[1]. When he receives the message from his friends in Varadin dungeon beseeching him to save them either by ransom or by deed of prowess, he does not hesitate a moment in his choice of the heroic alternative. He takes a desperate chance and braves the unknown in his assault on the mysterious mountain Vila, but he compels her to undo the mischief she has wrought, and gains her lasting allegiance. When he overcomes the monstrous, three-hearted Moussa[2]—thanks to a useful hint from his Vila friend—Marko grieves because he has slain a better man than himself. He is cunning and humorous in his adventure with Alil-Aga, and in the end shows himself a generous winner, although he cannot resist the temptation of reading the Turk a little lesson on the superior morality of the Serbs[3].

His delight in the wine-cup is unaffected and sincere. His manifold activities are punctuated by potations, his rough, cheery, convivial spirit is not to be denied. When the Sultan issues a decree forbidding wine to be drunk during the fast of Ramadan, Marko not only ignores the order but compels the gaping bystanders— the hodjas and the hadjis—to drink with him, for he cannot bear to drink alone[4].

His physical attributes are of the kind that win admiration in every country and in every age, and it is exceedingly probable that there is here a solid basis of fact and that here must be sought the origin of the Marko legend. His strength and skill in the use of weapons are marvellous. Philip, the terrible Magyar, smites the hero with his studded mace, and Marko scornfully begs him not to rouse the slumbering fleas, but when Philip's next blow breaks the golden goblet and spills the wine, Marko rises up in wrath and with one mighty sweep of his sword cuts the Magyar

[1] "A Damsel outwits Marko," p. 46, l. 84.
[2] "Marko and the Vila," pp. 21–24. A Vila comes to Marko's aid in "Musa the Outlaw," p. 124, ll. 234–245.
[3] "Marko and Alil-Aga," pp. 86–90.
[4] "Marko drinks Wine in Ramadan," p. 150. This bibulous trait emphasises the fact that Marko was no Turk.

in two[1]. His hand-grip is such that he can squeeze drops of water out of a piece of dry, hard wood: he overcomes a succession of the doughtiest champions, he fights victoriously against overwhelming odds, and, most wonderful of all, he pursues and captures the dangerous and elusive Vila of the mountain.

What an illuminating glimpse we get in Jevrosima's remark that she is utterly sick and weary of having to wash blood-stained garments. She suggests that her son should try ploughing for a change. Marko tries, in a grimly humorous way of his own, but his peaceful venture ends in a battle with Turkish janissaries. His amazing strength more than atones for his lack of weapons, for he whirls plough and oxen round his head, and with this original bludgeon beats the life out of his enemies[2].

Yet for all his courage and for all his strength, he is not always unflinching in fortitude nor supreme in the matter of thews and sinews. With true artistry the ballads tell how his spirit quailed in the frightful dungeon of Azak[3], how his courage halted in the presence of the Perilous Bogdan, how his strength was surpassed by that of Moussa the Outlaw. He is marvellous, indeed, but he is mortal man; he is portrayed neither as a god nor as an abstraction, and these deft touches which reveal his limitations and his weaknesses, serve but to reinforce his warm human vitality.

There remains the interesting question of his allegiance to the Sultan. How is it possible that the Serbs should have as their national hero one who was in the service of their mortal foe? The ballads themselves supply a partial answer. It is clear that the makers recognised the difficulty but turned it to their own advantage by a skilful reversal of the rôles, in such sort that Marko positively bullies his imperial master. That unhappy potentate usually brings the interview hurriedly to an end by plunging his hand into his "silken pocket" and presenting Marko with a fistful of ducats. One of several scenes of the sort takes

---

[1] "Marko and Philip the Magyar," pp. 78–83.
[2] "Marko's Ploughing," p. 158.
[3] "Marko in the Dungeon of Azak," pp. 107–111.

place when Marko kills the Turk whom he finds in possession
of his father's sword. On being made aware of the deed the
Sultan sends for his contumacious vassal. Marko stalks fiercely
into the presence and speaks the bold words: "If God himself
had bestowed the sword on the Sultan, I had slain the Sultan's
self[1]."

The problem really amounts to this—What were the special
qualities which gave Marko such a powerful hold on the imagina-
tion of his fellows? It must almost certainly have been his
possession of unusual physical strength and prowess, for it is
never claimed that he had intellectual gifts or that he was even
intelligent; he is described indeed as a "dunderhead[2]." Be that
as it may, the significant thing is that somehow or other he made
the necessary imaginative appeal, and his exploits as a Serb and
as a Christian became the theme of ballad minstrelsy. That the
guslari should extol their hero at the expense of the Turk was
only natural, they thus turned the tables, as it were, on their
conquerors.

Marko's fealty to the Sultan when thus manipulated and
adroitly combined with the suggestion that the nominal servant
was in reality greater than his lord, could prove no bar to his
popular acceptability. On the contrary, it was in this dual aspect
that he became the national hero, the ideal exemplar, the proud
symbol expressive of the unbroken spirit that lived on in spite
of disaster and defeat, and kept alive the confident hope that
however long the night, darkness must ultimately give place to
the dawn of another day.

There is nothing complex about Marko's character, his is
essentially a simple soul. There are no fine shades or subtle
distinctions. The contrasts are hard and violent, like the lights
and shadows of his native land. But he championed the oppressed

[1] "Marko recognises his Father's Sword," p. 70; "Marko's Hunting
with the Turks," p. 146; "Marko drinks Wine in Ramadan," p. 150.
[2] See "Marko's Hunting with the Turks," p. 146, ll. 31–32:

Али Марков соко јогуница
Као што је и негов господар.

Dickkopf is Dr Ćurčin's rendering of јогуница.

and defied the Turkish conqueror, and the simple peasants of his race have enshrined their simple hero in their heart of hearts[1].

In conclusion, something must be said about the verse in which the heroic ballads are composed, and the manner in which they are chanted by the bards. The poems consist of lines of ten syllables, unrhymed and with no "enjambement." Repetition, the fixed epithet and other devices are of constant occurrence and are often employed with telling effect. "Alles so wie in Homer" was Grimm's comment[2]. The bard or guslar is often blind, as by the best tradition it is fitting he should be, and his usual custom is to sit down under some shady tree where there is a good prospect of his having a sufficient audience. He then makes ready his gusle which in shape bears a rough resemblance to a mandolin, but the bridge rests upon a covering of vellum as in a banjo. The gusle is often adorned with carvings of kings and heroes. One in my own possession shows the figures of Tsar Lazar, Ivan Kosančić, Toplica Milan and others, the names being cut beneath them, while the neck of the instrument is carved to represent the neck and head of Šarac. The bow is in the shape of a curving snake and is strung with horsehair. Holding the gusle body downwards, the guslar fingers rapidly and draws his bow backwards and forwards across the single string, producing a weird wail that rises and falls. Then suddenly he plunges into his tale:

> Ili grmi, il' se zemlja trese?
> Niti grmi nit se zemlja trese,
> Već pucaju na gradu topovi,
> Ha tvrdome gradu Varadinu[3].

---

[1] During a visit to Belgrade, Kapper made the acquaintance of Knićanin, one of the Serb leaders in the revolution of 1848. Kapper records the conversation as follows. Knićanin asked—"'Kennt Ihr die Geschichte Markos?' Ich bejahte—'Seht Ihr, da kennt Ihr auch die ganze Geschichte des serbischen Volkes, und dann kennt Ihr auch das ganze serbische Volk selbst'" (*Südslavische Wanderungen*, vol. 1. p. 154).

[2] "It is clear enough that Servian heroic poetry bears little resemblance to the Homeric poems as we have them. But we may strongly suspect that at an earlier stage in the history of Homeric poetry the resemblance would be much closer...." Chadwick, *The Heroic Age*, p. 313.

[3] "Marko Kraljević and General Vuča," p. 49, ll. 1–4.

The ballads are not divided into separate verses or stanzas, but as a rule the minstrel pauses after every four or five lines and the plaintive cry of the gusle fills in the pause. It is as if one listened to the thin echo of the recitative, and in the proper surroundings the effect has an impressiveness of its own. Many peasants can perform creditably on the instrument, but naturally their repertoire is small compared with that of the professional bard who is now rarely met with in Serbia[1]. That, at least, is my own experience, for during a stay of some four years in the course of which I had occasion to travel through the greater part of the country, I came across no more than three men to whom the term "Guslar" might properly be applied.

An interesting point arises in connection with the poems as chanted or even read aloud. The natural accentuation of the words has to yield to the exigencies of the metre in a very remarkable way, and it has been suggested that this marked peculiarity may have some bearing "on the unelucidated question of Greek accent and quantity[2]."

The epic songs fall into two divisions:

(a) Those having a long line of fifteen or sixteen syllables, caesura after the seventh or eighth syllable, and a short recurring burden or refrain (pesme dugog stiha).

(b) Those having a decasyllabic line, caesura after the fourth syllable, and no refrain (pesme kratkog stiha).

The former are the older of the two and date back at least as far as the fourteenth century. Only about a hundred have survived, whereas there are thousands of specimens of the decasyllabic poems now extant. The themes of the older verses reappear in many of the later ballads but it is important to note that, whereas the ten-syllable poems are known and sung every-

[1] Cf. *Slavische Volkforschungen*, by Dr Friedrich S. Krauss, ch. XI. p. 183 ff. "Vom wunderbaren Guslarengedächtnis."

[2] Owen Meredith, *op. cit.* Introd. p. xxxii. "The following words, for instance, if pronounced without reference to prosody, would be thus accentuated: I pŏnĕsĕ | trī tŏvără blăgă.

But when sung to the gouslé as a verse, they are to be scanned thus: I pŏnĕsĕ | trī tŏvără blāgă."

where today, all knowledge of the older forms has vanished completely from the popular memory and hitherto no satisfactory account has been given of how or when they thus sunk into oblivion. The decasyllabic poems as chanted today have been classified under the following groups or cycles:

(*a*) Non-historical. A small group consisting of fairy-tales and of Christian and pre-Christian legends.

(*b*) Historical. A very large group containing the following ballad-cycles:

1. The Nemanja cycle.
2.   ,,   Kossovo   ,,
3.   ,,   Marko   ,,
4.   ,,   Branković   ,,
5.   ,,   Crnojević   ,,
6.   ,,   Hajduk   ,,
7.   ,,   Uskok   ,,
8.   ,,   Montenegrin Liberation cycle
9.   ,,   Serbian   ,,   ,,

The history of the decasyllabic verse is obscure and difficult to trace. Professor Popović is of opinion that it did not derive directly from the sixteen-syllable line, but sprang originally from a now forgotten intermediate form of eleven or twelve syllables which had borrowed certain themes from the longer metres. The decasyllabic ballad appears to have arisen among the Uskoks of the Coastland, not earlier than the seventeenth century[1]. Thence, adding to itself in its progress, it passed successively to Bosnia, Herzegovina and Montenegro, and so at last into Serbia where, with the ballads of the great rising against the Turks, the truly national poetry was brilliantly completed and rounded off. The wheel had thus come full circle and the story of the traditional folk-song ends in the country where in its older form it had had its birth[2].

[1] Soerensen's detailed study of the rise of the short-line verse should be consulted. See Appendix, p. 179 f. for an additional note on the date of the ballads.

[2] See *Jugoslovenska Književnost*, by Professor Pavle Popović, to which I am indebted for the foregoing summary account of the "pesme dugog stiha" and the "pesme kratkog stiha." Chapter, "Pred novim vremenom. Narodna Poezija," pp. 55–68.

In translating these admirable ballads, I was faced with the
inevitable choice between a free metrical rendering and a more
accurate prose translation. I chose the latter, partly because I
hoped the book might prove useful to students of the Serbian
language and literature, and considered that a large degree of
literalness would more than counterbalance the accompanying
disadvantages. Moreover, it must be confessed, I had grave doubts
of my ability to write even tolerable verse in the required measure,
and a few tentative efforts in that direction tended to confirm my
diffidence. But as each line of the original makes complete sense
in itself it seemed possible to write a line-by-line prose translation
and yet keep closely to the text. There are two obvious dangers
to be avoided; one is "fine writing," the other is baldness. The
ballad is apt to suffer very severely under the touch of the
self-appointed embellisher, and Marko would undoubtedly
lose much of his naive fascination if the stark manner of his
presentment were unduly modified by the translator. Yet, on
the other hand, without the insistent haunting monotony of the
decasyllables and the incommunicable verbal cunning that is part
of their fabric, the too literal translator may find himself lapsing
into the second error, and which is the greater evil it is hard to
say. I have done my best to maintain a decent equilibrium
between the bald and the elaborate, for each, in its own degree,
does injustice to the art and to the austerity of the original. I am
indebted to my friends Professors Bogdan and Pavle Popović
for their assistance in elucidating knotty points and to
Mr Alexander Yovitchitch, Major Milan Yovitchitch and
Mr W. K. Holmes for help in reading the proofs.

Note (*a*). I have used throughout the text of Vuk, *Srpske Narodne
Pjesme*, vol. ii. The collections of Bogišić, the Brothers Jovanović
and the others have not been drawn upon.

Note (*b*). In vols. I and VI of Vuk's collection there are thirteen
additional Marko poems, but as it is generally recognised that the
pieces contained in the second volume are the best of their kind, are
fully representative of the character and exploits of Marko and form
a complete whole in themselves, I have limited myself to this material.
Over two hundred Marko ballads are in existence but they have never
been gathered together.

GLASGOW, *August* 1921.

THE MARRIAGE OF KING VUKAŠIN

Wizened Vukašin wrote a letter
In white Skadar on the Bojana,
And sent it into Hercegovina
To the white stronghold Pirlitor[1],
To Pirlitor over against Durmitor,
To Vidosava wife of Momčilo;
Secretly he wrote and secretly he sent to her.
In the letter thus he spake to her:
"Vidosava, wife of Momčilo,
What wilt thou in yonder ice and snow?   10
If from the Castle thou lookest up,
Thou hast naught that is fair to see
But only white Durmitor mountain
Arrayed in ice and snow,
In summer as in winter;
If from the Castle thou lookest down,
Yonder gloomy Tara floweth turbulent,
Rolling with it trees and stones;
No ford is there on Tara nor any bridge,
And round about are pine trees and rugged rocks,   20
Therefore do thou poison Vojvoda Momčilo,
Or poison him or betray him into my hands;
Come to me to the level sea-coast,
To white Skadar on Bojana;
I shall take thee for my true wife,
And thou shalt be Lady Queen.
Thou shalt spin silk on a golden spindle,
Silk shalt thou spin, on silk shalt thou sit,
Thou shalt wear velvet and brocade,
And all the broidery shall be of purest gold[2].   30

[1] "Some sing *Piritor* instead of *Pirlitor*. It is said that the ruins of this place are still standing" (Vuk's footnote).

[2] А још оно што жежено злато: it is difficult to grasp the exact meaning. In all probability it refers to embroidery worked in thread of gold.

How fair is Skadar on Bojana!
If thou lookest at the hills above the Castle,
Figs and olives are ever growing,
Vineyards also there are, rich in grapes,
And if thou lookest from the Castle downwards,
Yonder fair wheat waxeth,
And round about are green meadows
Wherethrough green Bojana floweth,
And therein swim fishes of every sort   39
That when thou wilt thou mayst eat of them fresh caught."
The letter came to Momčilo's wife,
Heedful she scanned the letter, the wife of Momčilo,
Heedful she scanned it and wrote another letter:
"O my Lord King Vukašin,
Not easy is it to betray Momčilo
Not easy to betray nor yet to poison him;
Momčilo hath a sister Jevrosima,
She maketh ready for him the lordly meals,
She tasteth the dish before him;
Momčilo hath nine dear brothers,   50
And twelve nephews—brothers' sons;
They serve the red wine to him,
They drink of each glass before him:
Momčilo hath a horse Jabučilo[1],
Jabučilo a wingéd horse,
That can fly whithersoever he will:
Momčilo hath a sword with eyes[2],
And feareth none save God only.
But hear me now King Vukašin,
Do thou gather together a mighty host,   60
And lead them forth to the level lake,
And lie in a bushment in the greenwood;

---

[1] Jabučilo: Vuk has a footnote which will be found at the end of
the ballad. It is too long for insertion here.
[2] "I do not know what 'a sword with eyes' means, nor could the singer
explain. Perhaps the expression refers to some coloured device represent-
ing eyes" (Vuk's footnote). The meaning seems quite clear.

A strange custom hath Momčilo,
Each holy Sunday in the morning
He riseth early and goeth on hunting to the lake;
With him he taketh his nine dear brothers,
And his twelve brothers' sons,
And forty henchmen from the Castle;
And when the eve of Sunday is come,
I will singe the wings of Jabučilo,   70
I will seal up the keen sword,
I will seal it fast with salt blood,
That it may not be drawn forth of its sheath:
Thus shalt thou slay Momčilo."
When this letter came to the King,
And he perceived what the writing told him,
He was filled with joy.
Straightway he gathered a mighty host,
And came with the host to Hercegovina;
He led them forth to the level lake   80
And lay in a bushment in the greenwood.
When now the eve of Sunday was come,
Momčilo went to his bedchamber
And laid him down on the soft pallet;
Soon after his wife entered in also,
But she would not lie on the soft pallet;
Down her cheeks she wept hot tears,
Wherefore Vojvoda Momčilo asked of her:
"Vidosava, my faithful wife,
What great grief is thine   90
That thou criest tears down?"
And Vidosava his wife made answer:
"Lord and Master Momčilo Vojvoda,
No ill-fortune is come upon me,
But I have heard a wondrous marvel,
I have heard—I have not seen—
That thou hast a horse Jabučilo,
Jabučilo a wingéd horse,
But on thy horse have I seen no wings,

And I believe it not—   100
Also I fear me that thou art in danger to perish."
Sage was Vojvoda Momčilo,
Sage he was, yet was he deceived,
And to his wife thus he spake:
"Vidosava, my faithful wife,
As touching that I will give thee easy comfort,
Right well mayst thou see the wings of Čile.
What time the first cocks crow,
Get thee forth to the new stable,
Then will Čile let grow his wings   110
And so mayst thou perceive them."
He said, and laid him down to sojourn among dreams.
Momčilo slept but his wife slept not,
On the pallet she listened
For the first cocks to crow;
And when the first cocks crowed,
She sprang from the soft pallet,
She lit the candle in the lantern,
She took with her tar and tallow
And straightway went to the new stable.   120
And in truth it was as Momčilo had spoken,
For Jabučilo did cause his wings to grow,
Down to his hoofs he caused his wings to grow;
Forthwith she smeared his wings,
With tallow and with tar she smeared them
And with the candle she set the wings on fire;
With fire she burnt them up, the wings of Jabučilo,
And what by fire she could not utterly destroy,
She bound up fast around his knees.
Thereafter she hied her to the armoury,   130
She took the sword of Momčilo
She dipped it in salt blood,
And returned to the soft pallet.
On the morrow when the dawn whitened,
Vojvoda Momčilo arose,
And to his wife Vidosava he said:

"Vidosava, my faithful wife,
I dreamed a strange dream last night.
A tuft of mist writhed out
From Vasoje's accursed country,   140
And twined itself round Durmitor;
Through the mist I took my way
With my nine dear brothers,
And the twelve brothers' sons,
And forty men-at-arms from the Castle;
In the mist, dear wife, we parted,
We parted and met no more.
God wot—this bodeth no good thing."
His wife Vidosava made answer to him:
"Fear not, dear my Lord,   150
A good hero hath dreamt a good dream;
Dreams are lies, God alone is truth."
Vojvoda Momčilo made him ready to go forth,
And he came down from the White Tower.
Nine dear brothers await him,
And twelve brothers' sons,
And forty soldiers from the Castle.
His wife led out the white steed,
They mount the good horses,
And fare forth to hunt by the lake.   160
When they were come to the lake side,
The mighty host encompassed them about,
And when Momčilo was ware of the host,
He pulled at the sword by his side,
But in no wise could he draw it,
It was as if rooted in the sheath.
Then spake Vojvoda Momčilo:
"Hear ye my brothers!
Vidosava—the she-hound—hath betrayed me,
So give me a sword of the best."   170
Quickly the brothers obeyed him
They gave him a sword of the best,
And Momčilo spake to his brethren:

"Hear ye, my dear brothers!
Do ye fall on the flanks of the host
And on the centre will I set on myself."
Dear God, great marvel it was!
A thing worthy indeed to be seen of any man,
How Vojvoda Momčilo hewed about him,
How he brake him a passage down the hillside;   180
The horse Jabučilo trampled down more men
Than Momčilo cut down with the sharp sword.
Yet evil fortune met him in the way,
For as he pressed towards Pirlitor,
There met him nine black horses
But of his brothers on them there was not one.
And when Vojvoda Momčilo perceived it,
The hero's heart brake
With grief for his born brothers;
His white hands grew feeble,   190
He might wield the sword no more;
Therefore he smote the horse Jabučilo,
With boot and spur he smote him,
For to make him fly to Castle Pirlitor.
But the good steed might not fly,
And Vojvoda Momčilo cursed him:
"Jabučilo, may wolves devour thee!
In sport we have flown from here together,
Not urged by need, but out of joy of heart,
And today thou wilt not fly!"   200
The brave steed whinnied and made answer:
"Lord and master Vojvoda Momčilo,
Curse me not neither urge me onward;
Today I cannot fly:
May God slay thy Vidosava!
She burned up my wings with fire,
And what with fire she could not utterly destroy
That she bound fast about my knees;
Flee thou, therefore, whithersoever thou mayst."
When Vojvoda Momčilo heard this,   210

Tears rolled down the hero's cheeks;
From Čilaš his horse he sprang,
In three bounds he gained the Castle,
But the Castle doors were bolted,
Bolted and barred.
Now when Momčilo perceived his straits,
He cried to his sister Jevrosima:
"Jevrosima, dear sister mine,
Let down to me a length of linen,
That I may escape into the Castle."   220
Through her tears, sister to brother answered:
"Brother, Vojvoda Momčilo,
How shall I let down a length of linen,
When my sister-in-law Vidosava,
My sister-in-law—thy faithless wife,
Hath bound my hair to a beam?"
Yet the sister's heart was compassionate,
Anguish was hers for her born brother,
She hissed like an angry snake,
She swung her head with all her strength,   230
That the hair was torn from out her head,
And remained on the beam;
She took a length of linen cloth,
She threw it down from the Castle wall,
Momčilo seized the end of linen,
And thus he scaled the Castle wall;
Yet a moment and he had leaped within,
But the faithless wife sped thither amain,
In her hands she bore a sharp sword,
And she severed the linen sheet above his hand;   240
Momčilo fell down from the Castle wall,
The King's henchmen await him,
And on swords and war-spears he fell,
On clubs and battle-maces,
At the feet of King Vukašin;
The King thrust at him with a war-spear,
And pierced him through the living heart.

Then Vojvoda Momčilo lifted up his voice and cried:
"I adjure thee, King Vukašin,
Take not to thyself my Vidosava   250
Vidosava my faithless wife,
For she will cause thee to lose thy head also;
Today she betrayeth me to thee,
Tomorrow she will betray thee to another;
Wherefore do thou take my dear sister,
Mine own dear sister Jevrosima,
She will be faithful to thee ever,
And will bear thee a hero like unto myself."
Thus spake Vojvoda Momčilo
Thus he spake compelling his spirit,   260
And when he had spoken he gave up the ghost.
When Momčilo was now dead,
The Castle gates were opened,
And Vidosava that she-hound went forth,
And gave welcome to King Vukašin.
She led him to the White Tower,
She made him to sit down at golden tables,
And feasted him with wine and brandy,
With lordly dishes and fine meats of every sort;
Next she goeth to the armoury   270
And thence brought him Momčilo's apparel,
Momčilo's apparel and his weapons.
And now behold a marvel!
That which had reached to Momčilo's knees
Trailed on the ground behind Vukašin;
What for Momčilo had been a fitting helmet
Came down on the shoulders of Vukašin;
What had been a fitting boot for Momčilo
Therein Vukašin could put both his legs;
What had been a fair golden ring for Momčilo   280
Therein Vukašin might place three fingers;
What had been a proper sword for Momčilo
Trailed on the ground an ell's-length behind Vukašin.
What had been a coat of mail for Momčilo

Beneath its weight the King cannot bear him up
Then cried King Vukašin:
"Avaj—by the dear God—woe is me!
Lo, what a wanton is this Vidosava!
If today she betrayeth such a knight of prowess,
Whose match there is not in all the world,   290
How should she not betray me tomorrow?"
He called his faithful servants;
They seized Vidosava the wanton;
They bound her to the tails of horses;
They drave them apart before Pirlitor,
And the horses rent her living body in sunder.
The King laid waste Momčilo's stronghold,
And took to him Momčilo's sister,
Called Dilber-Jevrosima—the Fair Jevrosima;
He carried her off to Skadar on Bojana,   300
And took her to be his wife;
And by her he begat fair offspring,
She bare him Marko and Andrea,
And Marko followed in his uncle's footsteps,
In the footsteps of his uncle Vojvoda Momčilo.

Jabučilo, the winged horse: "It is said that in a certain lake in this region there was a winged horse which used to emerge at night and cover Momčilo's mares as they grazed in the meadows by the lake-side. When he had covered a particular mare he would kick her in the belly in order to cause abortion and thus to ensure that no winged offspring should be foaled. On learning this Momčilo provided himself with drums, kettledrums and other noise-producing instruments. He then drove his mares down to the lake-side as usual, and, during the day, concealed himself close by. At nightfall the horse came up out of the lake and covered one of the mares. As he was about to come down from her, Momčilo began to make a tremendous noise with the drums and other instruments, whereupon the horse took fright and dashed off to the lake without attempting to procure abortion in the mare. The latter thus remained pregnant and in due course foaled the winged horse owned by Momčilo. In the various versions of the story Momčilo's horse is referred to as враңче (the black horse), дорат (the brown) and ђогат (the white). In the version here given it is called Jabučilo and for short Čilaš and Čile" (Vuk's footnote).

THE DEATH OF DUSHAN[1]

(Fragment)

STEPAN, the Serbian Tsar, fell sick
In Prizren, place of light and leading.
Sore sick he was and like to die.
When Roxanda, the Tsaritsa, saw it,
She wrote with a pen,
As she had been a man,
Three letters she wrote, yea and four,
And sent them to the four corners of the land,
To the princes thereof each in his degree:
And she summoned all the lords to her, saying: 10
"Hearken all ye our princes!
Sore sick is the Tsar Stepan,
Sore sick he is and like to die;
Hie ye therefore to Prizren Castle,
If ye would find the Tsar on live,
And hear what he will ordain,
And to whom he will entrust the Empire."
When the letters were gone forth everywhither,
All the lords understood the writing;
They made such haste as ever men might,   20
And came every one to Prizren Castle,
To Stepan the mighty Serbian Tsar,
And they reached the Tsar
While he was yet on live;
And there all the lords were gathered together.
And thither also was come King Vukašin,
He raised the Tsar from his bed of silk,
And upheld him in his silken arms,

[1] Dušan: the Croatian alphabet should have been used consistently throughout this translation, but a few of the more familiar names have been inadvertently transliterated. Thus Šarac and Miloš appear sometimes as Sharatz and Milosh.

And great tears rolled adown his face.
The Serbian Tsar looked round about him,   30
On all his lords he looked in turn,
And after he had looked, he spake and said:
"Dear kum[1], King Vukašin,
I give in trust to thee mine Empire,
In trust all my towns and castles
And all my company of knights,
Each in his due degree throughout mine Empire;
And I give in trust to thee my babe, Uroš,
That lieth now forty days in his cradle.
Do thou reign kum, for seven years,   40
And on the eighth give over to my son Uroš."
But King Vukašin made answer:
"Dear kum, Tsar Stepan,
Not for me thine Empire,
Not for me to play the ruler,
Since myself have a wayward son,
Mine own son, Kraljević Marko;
He goeth whither him listeth, asking leave of none,
And ever at his down-sitting he drinketh wine out of
      measure,
And ever he stirreth up brawl and conflict."   50
Tsar Stepan made answer to him again:
"Dear kum, King Vukašin!
If I have ruled all my knights
Throughout the length and breadth of mine Empire,
Canst thou not rule one that thyself hast begotten?
I give thee mine Empire in trust,
In trust all my towns and castles
And all my company of knights,
Every each of them throughout mine Empire;
And I give thee also my babe Uroš,   60
That lieth now forty days in his cradle;

[1] Kum is roughly the equivalent of our "sponsor" or "godfather."
The godfather is *kum* to the godson and vice versa. The relationship
extends also to their respective children. See Appendix, p. 184.

Do thou rule, kum, for seven years,
And on the eighth give over to my son Uroš."
Thus spake the Serbian Tsar Stepan,
Thus he spake being at the point of death,
And when he had thus spoken, he gave up the ghost.

*   *   *   *   *

Sixteen years he ruled
And did so oppress the people
That what they had of fine raiment,
What they wore of silk apparel 70
They must change for rough homespun.
When young Uroš of noble line was grown in stature
    and understanding,
He called his mother to him and said:
"Mother mine, Tsaritsa Roxanda,
Give me my portion of my father's substance[1]."
His mother answered him:
"Hearken, my son Uroš!
Substance there is, in sooth, but another hath it,
To wit, King Vukašin.
When thy father died, 80
On his death-bed he entrusted the Empire
Unto his kum, King Vukašin,
That he should rule for seven years
And on the eighth give over to thee the Empire;
And behold, he hath ruled sixteen years."

      [1] Lit. "bread."

UROŠ AND THE MRNJAVČEVIĆI[1]

FOUR camps[2] were pitched one by other,
On the fair plain of Kossovo,
By the white church of Samodreža[3]:
One was the camp of King Vukašin,
The second, that of Despot Uglješ,
The third of Vojvoda Gojko,
And the fourth was that of the Tsar's son Uroš.
These princes disputed concerning the throne,
And fain would each slay the other;   9
Fain would each thrust other through with a golden dagger,
For they knew not which of them was to receive the empire.
King Vukašin said: "It is mine!"
Despot Uglješ: "Nay, but it is mine!"
"Not so," says Vojvoda Gojko, "For it is mine!"
The young Tsarevitch Uroš held his peace.
The child held his peace—he said no word
Because he durst not before the three brothers,
The brothers, the three Mrnjavčevići.
King Vukašin wrote a letter,
He wrote a letter and sent a messenger   20
To the white town of Prizren,
To the protopope Nedeljko;
That he should come to Kossovo plain
To declare who is to receive the empire;
For he administered the Sacrament to the glorious Tsar,
He administered the Sacrament to him and confessed him,
And in his hands are the ancient books[4].

---

[1] The family name of King Vukašin; see Мрнавчева Градина (Vuk's *Dict.*).

[2] табор = a camp or army.

[3] Some sing "Gračanica" (Vuk's footnote).

[4] књиге староставне. Professor Pavle Popović informs me that "the ancient books" are supposed to mean the old Serbian biographies (Sava, Domentian, Danilo and others). As these books deal chiefly with

Despot Uglješ wrote a letter,
He wrote a letter and sent a messenger
To the white town of Prizren,   30
To protopope Nedeljko.
A third letter wrote Vojvoda Gojko,
And sent likewise an ardent messenger.
A fourth wrote Tsar's son Uroš,
He wrote a letter and sent a messenger.
All four wrote letters,
And despatched swift messengers,
Each keeping secret from the others what he did.
The four envoys met together,
In Prizren, the white city,   40
Before the dwelling of protopope Nedeljko.
But the priest was not there,
He was in church at morning service,
At morning service and the reading of the Liturgy.
Overweening were the ardent envoys
And froward of the froward;
They would not dismount from their horses,
But urged them into the church.
They drew their pleated whips
And smote protopope Nedeljko: 50
"Come hence, and quickly, protopope Nedeljko!
Hence, and quickly, to the plain of Kossovo,
To declare who is to receive the empire.
Thou didst administer the Sacrament to the illustrious Tsar,
Thou wert his confessor also,
And in thy hands are the ancient books.
Do thou hasten or thou wilt presently lose thy head!"
Protopope Nedeljko shed tears,
He shed tears and answered to them again:

the Nemanja dynasty and do not admit any rival claim to the throne,
Marko, as a loyal subject, gives no heed to the demand of his father and
uncles, but declares in favour of Uroš, the last of the Nemanjas. Vuk
(*Dict.*) suggests цароставне as a possible reading. Cf. *Jugoslovenska
Književnost*, pp. 8–10, 14.

"Get ye gone—froward of the froward,   60
When we have ended the service in the church
It will be made known who is to receive the empire."
And the messengers gat them forth.
And when they had finished God's service,
And were all come forth before the white church,
Protopope Nedeljko spake thus:
"My children—ye four messengers,
I indeed gave the Sacrament to the illustrious Tsar,
I gave him the Sacrament and I confessed him;
But as touching the empire I asked him nothing,   70
I spake only of the sins that he had sinned.
So go ye to Prilep town,
To the abode of Marko Kraljevitch,
To Marko, erstwhile my pupil;
From me he learned his letters,
He has been scribe to the Tsar,
In his hands are the imperial writings,
And he knoweth who should receive the empire:
Summon ye therefore Marko to Kossovo,
Marko will speak forth the truth   80
For Marko feareth none,
Save only the one true God."
The four messengers departed thence,
They departed thence to Prilep town,
To the white castle of Marko Kraljevitch.
And when they were come before the white castle,
They knocked on the door with the knocker.
Jevrosima, the old mother, heard the knocking,
And called her son Marko:
"Son Marko, my dear child,   90
Who knocketh on the door with the knocker?
Meseemeth they should be messengers from thy father."
Marko arose and opened the door,
The messengers inclined themselves before Marko:
"God be thy help, Lord Marko!"
And Marko caressed them with his hand:

"Welcome, my dear children,
Is it well with the Serbian knights,
And with the noble Tsar and King?"
The envoys bowed the head in reverence: 100
"Lord Marko Kraljevitch!
In health all are well but they are not accorded together;
Our lords have quarrelled bitterly together,
On the wide Kossovo plain,
By the white church of Samodreža.
They dispute together concerning the succession,
And fain would each slay other.
Fain would each thrust other through with golden dagger,
For they know not which should obtain the empire.
They summon thee to Kossovo plain   110
To tell them who is heir to the empire."
Marko entered his lordly manor,
And called Jevrosima his mother:
"Jevrosima, my dear mother,
Our princes have quarrelled,
On the wide Kossovo plain,
By the white church of Samodreža.
They dispute together concerning the succession,
And fain would each slay other.   119
Fain would each thrust other through with golden dagger,
For they know not which should obtain the empire.
They summon me to Kossovo plain,
To tell them who is heir to the empire."
Now although Marko sought ever to do the truth,
Yet did his mother, Jevrosima, exhort him!
"Marko—only son of thy mother,
If the milk wherewith I nourished thee is not to be accursed,
Do not thou bear false witness,
To pleasure either thy father or thy uncles,
But speak according to the judgment of the true God;   130
Lose not thy soul, my son;
Better it is to lose thy head,
Than to sin against thy soul."

Marko took the ancient books,
He made him ready and made ready Sharatz[1].
He leapt on the back of Sharatz,
And set out for Kossovo plain.
And when they were come to the King's tent
King Vukašin cried:
"Good fortune is mine, by the dear God!   140
Behold my son Marko!
He will say that the empire falls to me,
For from the father it will pass to the son."
Marko heard, but said nothing,
Nor turned his head towards the tent.
And when Vojvoda Uglješ perceived him,
Uglješ spake this word:
"Good fortune is mine! Behold my nephew!
He will say that the empire falls to me.
Say, Marko, that the empire is mine   150
And we twain shall reign like brothers!"
Marko held his peace, he said nothing,
Nor turned aside his head to the tent.
And when Vojvoda Gojko perceived him
Gojko spake this word:
"Good fortune is mine! Behold my nephew!
He will say that the empire falleth to me.
When Marko was yet a little child,
I cherished him tenderly;
I folded him in my silken bosom   160
Like a fair golden apple;
And when I went forth on horseback
Ever I took Marko with me.
Say, Marko, that the empire is mine
And thou shalt reign chiefest therein,
And I will sit at thy knee."
Marko held his peace, he said nothing,
Nor turned his head towards the tent.
But he went straight to the white tent,

1 Šarac, the name of Marko's wonderful piebald horse.

To the tent of the stripling Uroš.   170
He urged Sharatz to the tent of the Tsar
And there Marko dismounted from Sharatz.
When the youthful Uroš perceived him
Lightly he leapt from the silken divan,
Lightly he leapt and cried:
"Fortunate am I! Behold my godfather!
Behold my godfather, Kraljevitch Marko!
He will declare who is to have the empire."
They opened their arms, they embraced,
They kissed each the other,   180
Each asked how it fared with other,
Then they sate them down on the silken divan.
And after a while
Day went; dark night came down.
Early in the morning when it dawned,
And the bells before the church were sounded[1],
All the princes came to the morning service.
And when they had finished service in the church,
They came forth out of the white church
And sate them down at tables before the church,   190
Sugar they ate and rakia they drank.
Marko took the ancient books,
He scanned the books and thus spake Marko:
"O King Vukašin, my father![2]
Is thy kingdom too small for thee?
Is it too small? May it become a desert!
Ye dispute now an empire that is another's.
And thou, uncle, Despot Uglješ[2],
Is thy domain too small for thee?
Is it too small? May ye lose it!   200
Ye dispute now an empire that is another's.
And thou, uncle, Vojvoda Gojko[2],
Is thy Vojvodstvo too small for thee?
Is it too small? May ye lose it!

---

[1] The bells were hung on a wooden framework outside the building.
[2] Vukašin, Uglješ and Gojko were all slain at the Marica (1371).

Ye dispute now an empire that is another's.
Look ye now, else may God not regard you!
The record saith that the empire goeth to Uroš,
From the father it descendeth to the son,
To the child the empire belongeth by heritage,
To him the Tsar bequeathed it,   210
When he died and went to his rest."
When King Vukašin heard this
The King sprang to his feet from the ground
And drew his golden dagger,
For to slay his son Marko.
Marko fled from before his father.
For it had ill become him, brother,
To fight with his own father.
Marko fled round the white church,
Round the white church of Samodreža.   220
Marko fled and the King pursued after him
Until they had thrice made a circle
Round the white church of Samodreža.
Almost had the King reached him,
When a voice spake from the church:
"Flee into the church, Kraljevitch Marko,
Dost thou not see that thou wilt perish this day,
Perish by the hand of thine own father
And that because thou hast spoken the judgment of
      the true God?"
The church door opened,   230
Marko fled into the white church;
Behind him the door closed.
The King rushed upon the church door,
He smote the wood with his dagger
And lo, blood dripped from the wood.
Then the King repented him
And spake these words:
"Woe is me, by the one God!
I have slain my son Marko!"
But a voice spake from the church: 240

"Hearken thou—King Vukašin,
It is not Marko thou hast stabbed,
But thou hast stabbed one of God's angels[1]."
Then the King was very wroth with Marko,
And in wrath he cursed him:
"Son Marko, may God slay thee,
Mayst thou have neither grave nor posterity,
And may thy soul not leave thee,
Until thou hast served the Turkish Sultan!"
The King cursed him, the Tsar blessed him: 250
"Marko, my godfather, may God be thy stay!
May thy face shine in the council-chamber!
May thy sword be sharp in the battle!
May no knight be found to put thee to the worse!
Be thy name renowned everywhere,
Whilst sun and moon endure!"
Thus they spake curse and blessing, and so also it
        came to pass.

---

[1] There is a flavour about this passage, unique in the Marko poems. The same sort of mysticism, however, informs certain portions of the Kossovo cycle.

MARKO KRALJEVIĆ AND THE VILA[1]

Two pobratims rode on the way together,
 Over fair Miroč mountain;
Kraljević Marko was the one,
The other was Vojvoda Miloš[2];
Both of them rode on noble steeds,
Both bore their battle-spears,
And each kissed the white face of other
For the love that is between two pobratims.
Sleep drew nigh to Marko as he sat on Sharatz,
And to his pobratim[3] he said: 10
"Ah, my brother, Vojvoda Miloš!
Sleep sits heavy on mine eyelids,
Sing to me, brother, and refresh me."
But Vojvoda Miloš made answer:
"Ah, my brother, Kraljević Marko,
Fain would I sing to thee, brother,
But last night I drank much wine
With Vila Ravijojla on the mountain,

---

[1] Vila: a species of nymph that haunted the wooded mountain-slopes and frequented springs. In Serbian song Vilas are represented as jealous and capricious beings but on the whole not unfriendly to mankind. They are still believed in by the peasants. A man who was in the service of my wife's family in Serbia saw a Vila on several occasions, and was reduced each time to a pitiable state of terror, from which I gather that the kind things said of them may be merely lip-service, an attempt to propitiate; cf. our "good folk."

[2] Miloš Obilić.

[3] Pobratim, lit. half-brother. When two men, not related, swear everlasting friendship, each becomes pobratim to the other. Formerly this was a very sacred alliance. For a wonderful description of the mystical nature of the bond, see *Večnost* by Janko Veselinović (Clarendon Press, 1918).

Posestrima is the corresponding feminine form. The vanquished Vila became Marko's "sworn sister." See "Musa the Outlaw," also "Leka's Sister," l. 408.

And the Vila laid threat upon me,
If she should hear me sing,   20
She will shoot me with arrows,
Through throat and living heart."
But Kraljević Marko answered:
"Sing, brother! fear not thou the Vila,
Since I, Marko Kraljević, am beside thee,
With my wonder-horse Sharatz
And my golden mace."
Then Miloš began to sing,
He began a beautiful song,
About all our best and oldest   30
Who held the kingdom,
And in Macedonia the fortunate
Raised pious edifices.
The song pleased Marko,
He leaned back on the pommel of the saddle,
He fell on sleep, but Miloš ceased not from singing.
The Vila Ravijojla heard him,
And began to join in the singing;
Miloš sang, the Vila sang against him,
But more beautiful is the voice of Miloš   40
More beautiful than the voice of the Vila;
Therefore the Vila Ravijojla was moved to anger,
She leapt down on the Miroč mountain,
She bended her bow and loosed two white arrows;
One arrow smote Miloš in the throat,
The other pierced his heroic heart.
Miloš cried: "Woe is me, my mother!
Ah me, Marko, brother-in-God!
Ah me, brother, the Vila has pierced me with arrows!
Did not I tell thee   50
That I might not sing on Miroč mountain?"
Marko roused himself from slumber,
And sprang from his piebald steed.
He pulled tight the girths of good Sharatz,
He embraced his horse Sharatz and kissed him:

"Alas, Sharo[1], thou my right wing!
If thou overtake the Vila Ravijojla,
I shall shoe thee with pure silver,
With pure silver and with beaten gold;
I shall cover thee with silk to the knees,   60
And tassels shall hang from thy knees to thy hoofs;
I shall mingle thy mane with gold,
And shall adorn thee with little pearls;
But if thou overtake not the Vila,
I shall put out thy two eyes,
And break all thy four legs,
And thus I shall leave thee
To drag thyself from pine to pine,
Like me, Marko, without my brother."
He leapt upon the back of Sharatz,   70
And dashed over Miroč mountain;
The Vila flew to the summit,
Sharatz galloped on the mountain slopes,
Nowhere saw he the Vila nor heard her.
But when at last he espied her,
He bounded into the air three spear-lengths,
Three spear-lengths high and four good spear-lengths
    forward,
And quickly Sharatz overtook the Vila.
When the Vila perceived her straits,
She flew upwards to the clouds in her distress,   80
But Marko drew his mace,
And hurled it strong and ruthless,
He smote the white Vila between the shoulders,
And felled her to the black earth.
Then he began to smite her with the mace,
He turned her to the right and to the left
And beat her with the golden mace.
"Wherefore, Vila—may God smite thee!—
Wherefore didst thou pierce my brother with arrows?
Give healing herbs to this worshipful knight,   90

[1] An endearing contraction of Šarac.

Else dost thou lose thy head!"
The Vila began to call him brother-in-God:
"Brother-in-God, Kraljević Marko!
Brother-in-God-the-Highest, and in Saint John!
Let me go forth alive into the mountain,
That I may pluck herbs on Miroč,
Wherewith to heal the hero's wounds."
And Marko was merciful for God's sake,
His heroic heart was compassionate,   99
He suffered the Vila to go forth alive into the mountain,
And the Vila gathered simples for Miloš;
The Vila gathered them, and ever and oft she called:
"I am coming, brother-in-God!"
The Vila gathered simples on Miroč
And healed the wounds of the hero.
More beautiful was now the voice of Miloš,
More beautiful than it had ever been.
And the heart of the knight
Was sounder than ever tofore.
The Vila hied her to the Miroč mountain,   110
Marko and his pobratim gat them on their way.
They journeyed even unto Porec.
They forded Timok river,
They came to Bregovo—the great village,
And fared onwards to Widdin.
And thus the Vila spake to her sister Vilas:
"Hearken unto me, ye Vilas,
Loose not your arrows against knights in the mountain.
If ye hear aught of Marko Kraljević,
Or of his magic horse[1], Sharatz,   120
Or of his golden mace.
What did not I suffer at his hands!
And hardly might I save myself alive!"

[1] Видовит: it is impossible to translate this word. In his *Dictionary*
Vuk says it is applied to children born with a caul. Such children when
they grow up know more than other folk and are able to consort with
Vilas. The same curious expression occurs in line 26.

MARKO KRALJEVIĆ AND THE
PERILOUS BOGDAN

EARLY one morn three Serbian Vojvodas
    Journeyed from Kossovo toward the rocky sea-coast.
One was Marko of Prilep,
The second was Relja of Pazar,
The third Miloš of Pocerje.
They took their way near by a vineyard,
That 'longed unto Bogdan, a full perilous knight.
Now Relja of Pazar spurred his horse,
And urged him through the vineyard,
And brake and did scathe in the rich vineyard.   10
Therewithal spake Marko to him, saying:
"Get thee forth of the rich vineyard, Relja!
Hadst thou known whose is this vineyard
Thou hadst ridden thy horse a great way round,
For it 'longeth unto the Perilous Bogdan.
Once afore I passed this way,
I brake and did scathe in the rich vineyard,
And the Perilous Bogdan perceived and saw me,
On his slender Arab mare he rode,
And I durst not await Bogdan,   20
But fled by the rocky shore;
The Perilous Bogdan pursued after me
On his slender Arab,
And but for my war-horse Sharatz,
Of a surety had he taken me.
But my Sharatz drew ever forward,
And the mare began to fall behind.
And when the Perilous Bogdan saw it,
He drew his heavy mace,
And hurled it after me by the rocky shore,   30
And smote me on the silken girdle.
With the mace-handle, pobratim, he smote me,

And dashed me on to the ears of Sharatz,
That scarce might I recover seat,
And escape along the rocky shore.
That is seven years agone,
Since then have I passed this way no more."
They held talk of this matter,
When there arose a cloud of dust,
And it came to the vineyard by the level shore.   40
The three Serb knights looked up,
And lo! the Perilous Knight was there,
With a fellowship of twelve knights with him.
And when Marko Kraljević saw it,
He spake unto Relja and unto Miloš, saying[1]:
"Hearken ye, my two pobratims!
See where he comes, the Perilous Knight!
Meseemeth all three we should lose our heads,
But come, let us flee hence[2]!"
But Miloš spake and said: 50
"Pobratim, Kraljević Marko!
Today folk deem and say also,
That three better knights of prowess are not,
Than we three Serbian Vojvodas.
Better were it for us three to perish,
Than that we should flee shameful this day."
When Marko heard it,
He spake unto them again, saying:
"How would ye that we divide them?
Whether would ye have ado with Bogdan alone,   60
Or with his twelve Vojvodas?"

[1] Relja: the winged Relja of Novibazar appears again in the story of Leka's sister. So also does Miloš of Pocerje who is the same as Miloš Obilić.

[2] This is one of the occasions on which Marko shows weakness. Goethe asked Talvj to omit "Лутица Богдан" from her translations: "denn hier erscheint Marko seiner unwürdig." For once Talvj did not agree: "Wenn ich das meinige tue den häszlichen Helden Marko berühmt zu machen, ihn beliebt machen, zu wollen, kann mir nicht einfallen." (Ćurčin, pp. 139–140).

Miloš and Relja answered him:
"We would have ado with Bogdan alone."
Marko had joy of that word,
And in the same hour Bogdan made onset.
Marko drew his heavy mace,
And drave the twelve Vojvodas before him.
He turned him about once and again,
And lo, he had stricken all twelve from their horses!
Right so he bound their hands,   70
And drave them round the vineyard.
And behold there was the Perilous Knight,
Driving tofore him Relja and Miloš,
And the hands of both he had bound.
And when Marko saw it,
He was afeared as never before,
And he began to look whither he should flee.
But on a sudden him remembered,
How each had sworn to other,
That if one should be in straits,   80
The others should come to his aid and comfort.
So he drew tight the reins of Sharatz;
He pulled down his sable kalpak on his forehead,
Until the fur made one with his eyebrows.
Then he drew his well-wrought sabre,
And looked darkly upon Bogdan;
Bogdan stood still by the vineyard,
But when he saw the black eyes of Marko,
And saw what was writ therein,
His legs were as palsied under him.   90
Marko looked at the Perilous Bogdan,
Bogdan looked at Kraljević Marko,
But neither would have ado with other.
At the last Bogdan spake and said:
"Come, Marko, let us leave this even hand.
Loose thou my twelve Vojvodas,
That I may loose unto thee Relja and Miloš."
Of that word Marko had great joy,

Straightway he loosed unto him his twelve Vojvodas,
And Bogdan loosed Relja and Miloš.   100
Then Marko took the wine-skin from Sharatz,
And sat him down for to drink rosy wine,
And he did eat also of the grapes of the vineyard.
And when they were merry with wine,
The three Serbian knights arose,
And took their good steeds.
And Marko spake to Bogdan and said:
"God abide with thee, thou Perilous Knight!
May we meet together in health yet again,
And toast each other in red wine."   110
But the Perilous Bogdan made answer:
"God go with thee, Kraljević Marko!
But may mine eyes see thee no more.
In such wise hast thou assailed me this day,
That never shall I yearn after thee to see thee."
Marko went up by the rocky shore,
Bogdan abode by his vineyard.

THE SISTER OF LEKA KAPETAN[1]

FROM the world's creation,
No greater marvel hath been,
Nor hath nowhere been heard tell of,
Than the marvel they say at Prizren,
Of the household of Kapetan Leka;
And the marvel they say is of the maid Rosanda.
God! How fair she is, may no ill befall her!
In the four quarters of the earth,
In all the lands of Turk and of Giaour,
There was not her like for beauty in the whole world,   10
Neither white Turkish maid nor Vlach,
Nor yet no damsel of slender Latin breed.
They that had seen the mountain Vila
Said that the Vila, brother, might not compare with her.
The maid grew up in a cage[2];
Fifteen years, they say, she dwelt encaged,
And saw not the sun nor yet the moon,
And the marvel was bruited through the world.
The tale went from mouth to mouth,
Until they heard it in Prilep;   20
And Marko Kraljević, the hero, heard it.
And it pleased Marko passing well,
That they praised her and spake no ill of him,
And him seemed that if she should be his wife,
Then Leka would be to him a worthy friend,
With whom he might drink wine

---

[1] "Captain" is not a suitable translation. Something equivalent to "governor" would be appropriate, but I have left the title "Kapetan" as in the original.

[2] у кавезу: perhaps not so figurative as it seems considering the way in which women were guarded. The same thing is referred to in the fairy-tale "Чардак ни на небу ни на земљи" which begins "Био један Цар, па имао три сина и једну кћер, коју је у кафезу хранио и чувао као очи у глави." Српске Народне Приповијетке, p. 7 (Биоград 1897).

And hold knightly converse withal.
Marko called his sister to him:
"Go, hasten, sister, to the čardak[1],
Open the box that is there,   30
And take out my finest apparel,
That I have made ready, sister,
For to put on against I marry me.
Methinks, sister, I go forth today
To Prizren under Šar mountain,
For to ask the maid in marriage of Leka;
And when I have won her, and brought her home,
Then will I marry thee, sister."
Quickly his sister ran to the čardak
And opened the box in the čardak   40
And took out the fine apparel.
And when Marko clothed him,
He put on cloth of velvet,
And on his head he set a kalpak with a silver crest,
And on his legs breeches with clasps,
Each clasp worth a golden ducat.
And he girded on his damascened sabre,
Whereof the golden tassels went to the ground;
Sheathed in gold was the sabre,
Sharp of blade and sweet to handle,   50
And the servants[2] brought out his horse,
And saddled him with a gilded saddle,
And put trappings on him that came down to his hoofs,
And over all a dappled lynx-skin,
And they bridled him with a bit of steel.
Now was Marko ready to depart,
He called his servants, the cellarer makes such speed as he may.
Between them they bear forth wine,
Two vessels of red wine,
One they gave to the war-horse   60

[1] Čardak: an upper-chamber (or a tower) with a verandah.
[2] I believe the word слуга might often be appropriately rendered as "squire."

That he grew blood-red to the ears.
The second Marko drank as stirrup-cup,
And he grew blood-red to the eyes.
And now dragon rode forth on dragon[1],
And they went out over the fields of Prilep.
So they passed over hill and dale
And drew nigh to Kossovo.
But Marko would not to level Mitrovica,
But turned him aside at the first cross-roads,
And went straight to his pobratim,   70
To his pobratim Vojvoda Miloš.
And when Marko was come near to the castle,
Vojvoda Miloš perceived him,
From his white tower he saw him,
And called to him his many servants:
"Servants mine, open the gate!
Get ye out to the wide plain,
Go by the broad highway,
Your caps, children, put under your armpits,
And do obeisance down to the black earth,   80
For lo, my pobratim Marko cometh to me!
Lay not hold on the hem of his mantle,
Offer not to bear his sword for him,
Nor go ye too nigh to Marko,
For it may be that he is in anger,
It may be that he is flown with wine,
And well might he trample you under his horse's feet,
And leave you, children, in evil case.
But when Marko is come in at the gate,
And we have embraced each the other,   90
Then take ye Marko's horse,
And I shall lead Marko to the čardak."
Quickly the servants set open the gate
And met Marko in the field.

---

[1] А кад ала алу појахала. "Ала" according to Vuk (*Dict.*) is a kind of dragon which has the power to bring clouds and hail. Here, of course, figurative, meaning "mighty one."

But Marko looked not at the servants,
But rode his ways past them;
He rode his horse to the gate,
And at the gate he lighted down.
The Vojvoda Miloš came forth,
And met Marko his pobratim;   100
They spread out their arms and kissed each the other,
And Miloš would fain have led him to the čardak,
But Marko refused and would not to the čardak.
"Nay, brother," quoth he, "I will not to the čardak,
I have no time for feasting;
But whether hast thou heard,
Concerning Prizren the white city,
And the household of Kapetan Leka?
For thereof they say great marvel.
Wondrous marvel they say of the maid Rosanda;   110
In the four quarters of the earth
In all the lands of Turk and Giaour,
There be none like unto her in the whole world.
Neither white Turkish maid nor Vlach,
Nor yet no damsel of slender Latin breed.
They that have seen the mountain Vila,
Say that the Vila, brother, may not compare with her.
Thus folk praise her, and no man sayeth aught against us.
Today we two pobratims
Have met together, both of us unwed,   120
Unworthier men have made mock of us,
Less worshipful than we have wedded,
Yea, and have begotten offspring,
And we remain, brother, for a reproach!
We have a third pobratim,
The winged Relja of Pazar;
Beyond Raška, beyond the cold river.
From the first we have been true brethren.
Put on now thy finest apparel,
Take with thee gold also,   130
And take a golden ring for the maiden;

We shall ask the winged Relja to go with us,
And when we are safe come to Prizren,
Let Leka and the maid look upon us;
Let her choose which of us she will,
And that one shall be the happy bridegroom,
And the other twain shall be the two devers[1],
And all three of us shall be Leka's chiefest friends."
Miloš heard it and it liked him well,
He left Marko in the courtyard,   140
He gat him to the slender čardak,
And put on splendid apparel;
A sable kalpak with a silver crest that turned like a wheel,
And garments of many folds,
And over all he donned a gay mantle,
Such as today no king possesseth.
There was paid thirty purses of gold
For the lining within,
As for the outside, none may tell
The gold that it cost.   150
The servants led forward his swift steed[2].
Now whilst Miloš garbed him,
Marko was drinking wine;
One great vessel full of wine he drank,
And his horse drained another.
Ah, hadst thou but seen with thine eyes,
Hadst thou but seen the Vojvoda Miloš!
Marko was as naught
Compared with Miloš the Vojvoda.
For none was of greater stature,   160
There was none more broad of shoulder;
And what a knightly aspect was the hero's!

---

[1] Dever: bride-leader, paranymph. Corresponds roughly to "best-man." Cf. Gk. δαήρ, Lat. levir.

[2] А слуге му ждрала изведоше: "And the squires led out his crane." The crane is regarded as typical of gracefulness, and a fine-looking horse is often called "a crane" (ждрал) or is referred to as ждралин, "swift steed."

What a pair of eyes he had!
What a mighty black moustache!
Graceful it drooped to his shoulders;
Happy she that taketh him to husband!
And now they mounted their good steeds,
And went forth to Mitrovica plain.
They descended towards Novi Pazar,
Along the Raška to Relja's manor.   170
Relja saw them and came out to meet his pobratims,
They spread wide their arms and kissed one the other.
In the gateway they lighted down,
And swift squires took the horses.
Then Relja bade them to the čardak,
But Marko would not, and he said to Relja:
"We will not, pobro, to the čardak,
Nor to the čardak nor to the slender tower."
And he told him all wherefore they journeyed.
"Come, Relja," quoth he, "Come, pobratim,   180
We shall wait for thee a little:
Put on thy finest raiment upon thee,
And let the servants saddle thee thy horse."
Relja was glad of that word.
Hadst thou but seen with thine eyes
When the winged hero donned his apparel!
Hadst thou seen the splendid bridegroom
That the winged Relja made!
It is no jest that the hero had wings,
No jest is it—he had wings indeed.   190
A sorry figure was Marko beside him,
A sorry figure also Miloš the Vojvoda.
Relja mounted his Vila-steed[1],
And they went by the wide plain,
Along the Raška, by the cold river.
And they came to the fords,
And they crossed the Jošanica water,

[1] Виловита коња појахао: to express the superlative quality of his horse, the Vila being endowed with marvellous swiftness.

Seven and seventy fords[1].
They reached Kolašin village
And went down to level Metohia.   200
They came to Senovac village,
To Senovac and so to Orahovac;
Then they went over level Metohia,
And entered on the Prizren plain,
Under high Šar mountain.
And they were yet afar off,
When Leka Kapetan espied them.
He took his spy-glass of crystal,
That he might see who they were and whence,
For Leka Kapetan wit well   210
That they were worthy knights and horses;
And when he put the spy-glass to his eye,
Forthwith he knew the three Serbian Vojvodas,
He knew them and marvelled,
And also was he somewhat adread.
And Leka cried with a loud voice,
With a loud voice he cried and called his servants:
"Servants mine, open the gate!
Servants mine, haste ye forth into the field!
There come to me three Serbian Vojvodas.   220
I know not what this portendeth,
Nor know I whether there will be peace in our land."
Quickly the servants set open the gate,
And went forth afar over the plain,
And they bowed them down even to the ground,
But the Vojvodas regarded not the servants,
But urged their horses onward to the gate.
There the servants drew nigh to them,
And took their valiant steeds,

[1] "Seven and seventy": probably to express an indefinitely large number. "Two and twenty" is frequently used in this sense. Cf. the words of the kolo song beginning: " Igra kolo, igra kolo na dvadeset i dva." In the *Iliad* a very long spear is δυοκαιεικοσίπηχυ (xv. 678), and a huge bowl is δυοκαιεικοσίμετρος (xxiii. 264). Cf. also l. 345 of this ballad and page 141 line 99.

And Leka Kapetan came forth; 230
In the courtyard he met the three Vojvodas,
They halsed each other in arms and kissed each the other,
And each hero asked other how he did;
Each took other by the hand,
And went, brother, to the slender čardak.
And when they were gone up into the čardak,
Albeit Marko had gone to and fro in the earth,
Nor marvelled no more at anything,
Nor was never abashed,
Yet here Marko both marvelled and was abashed, 240
When he beheld Leka's čardak,
And saw the splendour thereof.
Wherewith, think ye, was the floor covered?
With fine cloth that reached to the door of the čardak;
And on the cloth was spread fair velvet.
And how, think ye, were the beds in Leka's manor?
How the pillows under the head?
All, all were wove in thread of purest gold.
Round the čardak were pegs a many,
Wherefrom hung knightly weapons, 250
And the pegs were of white silver;
And the columns round about the čardak
Were all of white silver,
And the capitals thereof were of fine gold.
And on the left side of the čardak
Was the well-garnished sofra[1],
And along it wine had been poured out,
And brimmed in golden beakers;
And at the head thereof stood a goblet
That held full nine litres of wine, 260
And was wrought of purest gold.
It was the goblet of Leka Kapetan,
And of that Marko had great marvel.
And now Leka bade them sit down,
He made place at the head of the sofra,

[1] Sofra: the low table round which the guests squatted on cushions on the floor.

Gladly he welcomed the Vojvodas.
Therewithal came the swift servants,
They took the beakers from the sofra,
And gave them into the hands of the knights;
But first they gave to their own lord and master, 270
To Leka Kapetan their lord.
And wine there was out of measure,
And the sofra was garnished with all knightly cheer,
And with fine meats of every sort.
They drank wine, yea, and so they tarried
From Sunday again to Sunday,
And oft did Marko cast glance of eye
Upon his two pobratims,
For to know whether of them should speak to Leka,
And say the word concerning the damsel. 280
But when Marko looked at them,
They cast their eyes on the ground.
No light thing was it to speak of this matter to Leka,
That was such a great and worshipful knight.
When Marko saw himself in this strait,
He needs must speak the word to Leka:
"Most worshipful Leka," quoth he,
"We sit and we drink wine,
And we have spoken together of all matters,
And ever I look to thee and listen 290
When thou wilt ask me, Leka,
Wherefore we are come this far journey,
And wherefore we have tired our horses.
But thou wilt not ask me, Leka!"
And now indeed it was hero against hero,
And craft met craft again;
And Leka answered him right craftily:
"O Vojvoda, Kraljević Marko,
How should I ask thee, brother,
Since thou, Marko, hast long not honoured me? 300
Why are ye not oftener come to me
That each might ask how it fared with other,

That we might drink red wine,
And see if peace were to reign in the land?
Ye are come to me today, tomorrow I will go to you.
He said and waited the word of Marko;
Nor for long was Marko silent,
But made answer to him again:
"All is as thou sayest, Leka Kapetan,
But I have somewhat more to say unto thee   310
On a matter that is hard to open;
News of import hath reached us,
For they say that here is a marvel,
A wondrous marvel, even the proud maid Rosanda.
They say that in the four corners of the earth,
In Bosnia and in Rumelia,
In Syria and in Egypt,
In Atolia and in Anatolia,
And in the seven Vlach kingdoms,
And in the whole world none may compare with her. 320
They praise her, and no man sayeth aught against us.
We are come, Sir Leka,
That we may ask the maid in marriage;
All three we are pobratims,
All three till now unwed:
Give thy sister to which of us thou wilt,
Choose for brother-in-law which thou wilt,
That one may be the eager bridegroom,
And the others his two devers,
And that all may be thy chiefest friends."   330
Leka was angered and made frowning countenance;
"Think not of that," quoth he, "Vojvoda Marko!
Bring not forth a ring for the maid,
Nor yet the suitor's flagon[1].

---

[1] Просачка буклија: according to the custom, if Marko had produced the "suitor's flagon," and if Leka had drunk out of it, he would
have been pledged to see that his sister married one of the three heroes.
As he had no authority over his wilful sister he dared not enter into any
agreement on her behalf.

What I as a knight have sought of God,
That have I obtained this day
In that I gain for me such friends.
But I must tell you a hard thing;
Sooth it is that thou hast heard, Vojvoda Marko,
That there is no such damsel of beauty;   340
It is true indeed what folk say,
But this my sister is a shrew,
She feareth none save God,
She careth naught for her brother.
Four and seventy suitors there are,
That are come seeking my sister,
And in all my sister hath found some fault,
And shamed her brother before the suitors.
I durst not take thy ring,
Nor drink of the suitor's flagon.   350
If my sister will not go with you tomorrow,
How then shall I answer you?"
Into loud laughter brake Marko,
And spake to him in this wise:
"Ah me, Leka, alas for thy mother!
Art thou then head of this household,
And ruler of the level plain,
And thine own sister feareth thee not?
By the faith of my body,
Were it my sister in Prilep,   360
And she would not obey me,
I should cut off her hands,
Or put out her eyes!
But hear me now, Leka Kapetan!
And if thou art afeared of thy dear sister,
I pray thee as head of the household
That thou go to the white tower;
Go, Leka, where thy sister sitteth,
Ask her and bring her hither,
And let her look upon us knights;   370
It may well be that such she hath never seen.

Do thou tell thy sister, Leka,
That she may choose which of us she will,
And we brethren shall not quarrel,
But one shall be the bridegroom,
The other twain shall be the devers,
And we shall all be thine own good friends."
Up sprang Leka, no word he said,
He went to the high tower,
And spake to his sister Rosanda: 380
"Come, sister, come proud Rosa,
Come, sister, to the slender čardak!
It so fortunes thee in this thy life,
That of three Serbian knights thou mayst take thy choice,
Whose like there is not in the world this day;
Thereby shall thy brother gain good friends
And thou, sister, shalt wed with great honour."
The sister made answer to her brother:
"Go, brother, to the slender čardak,
Drink wine together and toast one the other,   390
Behold thy sister cometh to the čardak."
Forthwithal goeth Leka to the čardak,
And like brethren the knights sit together in the čardak.
Then a sound was heard in the high čardak,
There was a sound on the slender staircase
Of dainty slippered feet,
And lo, a bevy of maidens!
And in the midst thereof the maid Rosanda.
And when Rosanda entered into the čardak,
The four corners thereof glittered   400
With the splendour of her apparel,
And the beauty of her form and features.
The three Serbian knights looked upon her,
They looked and were abashed,
For in sooth they had great marvel of Rosa.
Many a wonder had Marko seen,
He had seen the Vilas of the mountains,
And he had Vilas that were his sworn sisters,

But never tofore had he been adread,
Nor never tofore had he been abashed.   410
Yet now of Rosa had he exceeding great marvel,
And in Leka's presence he was sore abashed,
That he cast his eyes upon the ground.
And Leka Kapetan perceived it.
He looked at his sister, he looked at the Vojvodas
For to see whether of the knights would speak,
Or with him or with the slender damsel.
But when he saw how the knights were silent,
He made the matter plain to his sister:
"Choose, sister," quoth he, "which thou wilt   420
Of these three worshipful knights.
And if thou art minded, sister,
To take a good knight of prowess,
That will make our face to shine with glory
On every field of strife,
One that cometh forth with worship from every tourney,
Take, sister, Kraljević Marko.
Go with him to Prilep castle,
It will be well with thee there.
But if, sister, thou art minded   430
To take the knight of fairest seeming,
Whom none may match for strength and comeliness,
Nor yet in stature nor in stoutness of countenance
In the four ends of the earth,
Then take, sister, the knight Miloš.
Go with him to the plain of Kossovo,
There too it will be well with thee.
But if, sister, thou art minded
To take a winged knight,
That thou mayst embrace him and be proud,   440
Take, sister, the winged Relja,
Go with him to Novi Pazar,
And there, too, it will be well with thee."
When Rosanda the damsel heard it,
She smote the palms of her hands together,

That the čardak rang in the four corners thereof;
And therewithal she began to speak shameful words:
"God be praised! Praise be to the true God!
I can understand marvels of every sort,
And for all adversities I can find a remedy.   450
But I understand not this land of Prizren,
That hath bestowed the rank of chief
On a madman like Leka Kapetan!
Where is thy understanding? Thou hast lost it!
What whim hath taken thee, brother?
How hast thou been so befooled this day?
Liever had I remain unwed[1],
In this our realm of Prizren
Than go to Prilep castle,
And be called Marko's wife.   460
For Marko holds of the Sultan,
He fights and smites for the Turks,
Never will he have grave nor burial,
Nor o'er his grave will burial service be read.
Wherefore with all my beauty should I be wife to a
        Turkish minion?
Yet would I not be angered,
That thou art deceived by reason of Marko's valour,
But I am wroth with thee,
That thou findest aught to love
In this Vojvoda Miloš,   470
Because he is featly fashioned of body and a strong knight.
Hast thou heard what folk say concerning him?
They say that a mare foaled Miloš[2],
A grey Arab mare,
An Arab mare that brought forth crane-like foals[3];
In the morning they found Miloš in the stud,
And the mare suckling him with her udder;

[1] Lit. "to comb my grey hair."
[2] The hero's surname Obilić was said by many to be Kobilić, and
as kobila = a mare, the point of the sneer is obvious.
[3] See note, line 151.

Hence his strength and his greatness of stature.
Yet even therefor should I not be wroth,
But this, brother, has moved me to anger,   480
That thou speakest to me of the winged Relja!
Where is thy understanding? Thou hast lost it!
Where is thy tongue? Thou speakest no word!
Wherefore, brother, askest thou not Relja
What is his parentage and what his line,
Who his father, and who his mother?
For I have heard folk say
That Relja is a bastard of Novi Pazar.
They found him one morning in the street,
And a gipsy suckled him.   490
Hence hath he his pinions;
I go not with him nor with any of them."
She said, and went down from the čardak.
Behind her, face flamed to face,
For the knights were shamed in each other's presence,
And Marko's anger blazed like living fire.
Lightly he leapt to his feet,
He snatched his sharp sword from the nail,
And would have stricken off Leka's head,
But Miloš sprang forward and seized Marko,   500
And grasped the sabre in his hand:
"Hold thy hand," quoth he, "Kraljević Marko,
Leave thy sabre—God's curse upon it!
Wouldst thou do scathe to this our brother
That hath so well received us?
And for a wretched she-bastard,
Wouldst thou make all Leka's land to weep?"
And Miloš suffered him not to lay hands on Leka.
Marko looked, and a thought came to him,
He sought no more to take his sabre,   510
But looked at the dagger in his girdle,
Then rushed down from the slender čardak.
And when Marko reached the ground,
And set foot on the stony pavement,

Rosa was nigh unto the tower,
And her maidens were round about Rosanda;
They upheld her flowing sleeves and the hem of her
      garments;
Marko saw it and cried aloud:
"O damsel, O proud Rosanda,
I beseech thee of thy youthfulness,   520
Send from thee thy maidens
And turn thy face to me!
For I was sore abashed, Rosa,
Before thy brother in the čardak
So that I saw thee not well.
And when I go to Prilep castle,
My sister will weary me
Asking: 'Was Rosa fair to look upon?'
Turn thee, that I may see thy face."
The damsel sent away her maidens,   530
She turned her about and showed her face:
"Now Marko," quoth she, "thou mayst look on Rosa!"
Marko raged and was wroth out of wit,
One step he made and a mighty spring,
And by the hand he seized the damsel,
He drew the sharp dagger from his girdle,
And cut off her right arm;
He cut off her arm at the shoulder,
And gave the right arm into her left hand,
And with the dagger he put out her eyes,   540
And wrapped them in a silken kerchief,
And thrust them into her bosom.
Then spake Marko in this wise:
"Choose now, thou maid Rosanda,
Choose now which thou wilt,
Whether the Turkish minion,
Or Miloš the mare's son,
Or Relja the bastard!"
Rosa shrieked that it was heard afar,
And she cried to her brother Leka: 550

"O my brother, Leka Kapetan!
Seest thou not how I perish miserably
At the hands of mighty Kraljević Marko!"
In the slender čardak Leka hears her,
But he is silent as were he a cold stone,
Nor durst he speak a word,
Lest he too should perish.
Marko lift up his voice, for he would not enter again
    into the čardak,
He called to his two pobratims:
"Come, brothers, come down from the čardak!   560
Bring my sabre in your hands,
The time is come for us to depart."
The pobratims hearkened unto Marko,
They came down to the pavement,
Marko girded on his sword below the čardak,
They mounted their good steeds,
And went forth over the wide plain.
Leka stayed like a cold stone,
And Rosa, mutilated, kept wailing.

A DAMSEL OUTWITS MARKO

THERE was a poor maid that was an orphan,
  When she dined then she supped not,
If she dined and supped
Then she had no clothing.
Yet for all that good fortune came to her[1],
Kraljević Marko sought her in marriage,
Vojvoda Janko urged a rival suit,
Pavle Ustupčić gave her a ring.
And the three suitors arose,
Each with a thousand wedding-guests with him,   10
And came right so to the damsel's dwelling.
Marko came first, and behind Marko, Janko,
And behind Janko, Pavle Ustupčić.
Kraljević Marko looked behind him,
And spake to the Vojvoda Janko:
"Whither goest thou, Janko?
Wherefore hast thou troubled so many guests,
And wearied so many horses,
Since that the maid is not for thee,
But for me, Kraljević Marko?"   20
Janko held his peace and said nothing,
But he turned him to Pavle Ustupčić
And spake to him (softly)[2], saying:
"Whither goest thou, Pavle?
Wherefore hast thou troubled so many guests,
And wearied so many horses?
Not for me the maiden, nor yet for thee,
But for the falcon, Marko Kraljević."
Pavle held his peace, he said nothing,

---

[1] The phrase "good fortune" when used with reference to a girl commonly signifies an offer of marriage.

[2] тихо or, as here, тиjо = lit. "softly." In the epic ballads, however, the word connotes no idea of a lowering of the voice, but indicates an ordinary speaking tone as distinguished from shouting. It should be omitted in translating.

But he rode forward before his wedding-guests.　30
And when they were come near to the house,
The maid's mother had seen them afar off,
And came forth joyfully to meet them.
Then she conducted the lordly throng,
And led them three by three into her dwelling.
The Kums[1] she set each by other,
The Stari Svats[2] each by other,
The suitors each by other.
After that she turned to the wedding-guests:
"Ye well-beseen guests," quoth she,　40
"Enter, good friends, an it please you!"
When the guests had rested them a little,
Marko Kraljević arose
And pulled out his damascened sabre,
And laid it across his knees.
Then he turned him to Janko,
And spake (softly) to him, saying:
"Hearken to me, Vojvoda Janko,
And thou likewise, Pavle Ustupčić!
We shall set out three golden apples[3],　50
And three golden rings;
Let them bring forth the fair damsel,
And let her choose whose apple she will,
Or apple or golden ring.
And he whose ring or apple she taketh,
Shall himself take the fair damsel."
Forthwithal they obeyed Marko,
They set out three golden apples,
And three golden rings;
Then the fair damsel was brought,　60
And Marko Kraljević spake, saying:
"Hear me, fair damsel,

[1] Kum = godfather, sponsor, principal witness.
[2] Stari Svat: lit. "the senior guest"; the meaning approximates
to "second witness."
[3] Ring and apple form part of the offering of a suitor. If the girl
takes the apple it is a sign that the suitor is accepted.

Choose now whose apple thou wilt have,
Or apple or golden ring."
When the damsel understood these words
(Though poor she was also prudent),
She answered him again, and said:
"Kum-in-God, Kraljević Marko[1]!
Stari Svat, Vojvoda Janko!
And all ye gay wedding-guests,   70
Brothers-in-God, good friends!
An apple is a toy for children,
But a ring is a knightly pledge.
I will wed with Pavle Ustupčić."
Marko roared like a beast of the forest,
He smote his knee with his hand,
And said to the poor maiden:
"Bitch that thou art!
Someone hath taught thee this,
But say now who hath taught thee!"   80
The damsel made answer:
"Dear Kum, Kraljević Marko,
Thy sword instructed me."
Then Marko laughed loudly upon her,
And spake to her, saying:
"Well for thee, fair damsel,
That thou tookest no apple,
Nor apple nor golden ring!
By the faith of my body,
I should have cut off thy two hands,   90
Nor wouldst thou have saved thy head,
Nor ever on thy head have worn the green garland![2]"

[1] When Marko laid his drawn sword across his knees the girl understood the hint perfectly. She was in love with Pavle, but she dared not choose his gift for, if she did, she knew that Marko would kill her. But her nimble wit enables her to evade the danger and at the same time to gain her heart's desire. She ignores the gifts and before the assembled wedding-guests hails Marko as her Kum and Janko as Stari Svat. By all the rules Marko is bound to accept office and *ex officio* it is his duty to further the marriage which he had been so eager to prevent.
[2] The wedding-wreath.

MARKO KRALJEVIĆ AND GENERAL VUČA

Is it thunder or is it earthquake?
No thunder is it nor yet earthquake[1];
They are firing the guns in the castle,
The strong castle of Varadin.
General Vuča maketh merry,
Because Vuča hath gained a victory.
He hath taken three Serbian Vojvodas.
The first is Miloš of Pocerje[2],
The second is Toplica Milan,
The third is Kosančić Ivan[3].   10
He hath flung them into the depths of a dungeon
Where the water cometh to their knees,
And the bones of dead heroes are shoulder high.
Miloš of Pocerje hissed forth lamentations,
Miloš hissed like an angry snake,
For Miloš had never learned
To endure suffering and evil fortune.
Miloš hissed like an angry snake,
He pulled himself up to the dungeon window,
And the hero looked out into the street   20
If haply he might see one known to him.
And he perceived a messager,
And Miloš of Pocerje called him, saying:
"Brother-in-God that bearest the letters,
Bring me a sheet of paper,
That I may make ready a letter."
"I will well," said the post,
And he brought him a sheet of paper.

---

[1] A common device in Serbian ballads. The attention of the listener
is arrested from the outset. The so-called "epic antithesis."

[2] Miloš of Pocerje is the same as Miloš Obilić.

[3] Toplica Milan and Kosančić Ivan are two heroes of the Kossovo
cycle. Miloš, Milan and Ivan were all present at the Slava celebrated
by Tsar Lazar at Kruševac before the battle.

Miloš sate him down and wrote a letter,
To Prilep the white castle,   30
To Marko Kraljević, his pobratim:
"Brother-in-God, Kraljević Marko,
Hast thou not heard—or carest thou naught for me?
Into sore straits am I come,
In the hands of the Magyars.
General Vuča hath taken me,
And with me my two pobratims.
He hath cast us into the depths of a dungeon,
Where the water cometh to our knees,
And the bones of dead heroes are shoulder-high.   40
Three white days have I lain here, brother,
And, brother, if I remain yet three days,
Nevermore shalt thou see me!
Deliver me, pobratim Marko,
Be it with gold or by deed of prowess."
Then he struck the pen into his face,
And caused the blood to pour from his cheek,
With blood he sealed his letter.
He gave it to the post,
And gave him twelve ducats,   50
And to the post Miloš saith:
"Bear this letter to white Prilep,
To the knees of Kraljević Marko."
The post departed for white Prilep,
And reached it on the holy Sabbath,
What time the Serbs were at church.
The post stood before the white church,
Until Marko should come forth of the church;
And anon when Marko came forth,
The post set his cap under his arm,   60
And bowed to the ground before Marko,
And gave him the letter.
When Marko received the letter,
Standing, Marko oversaw the letter,
And when he perceived what it told him,

Tears came into his eyes,
And he lift up his voice and cried:
"Woe is me, my dear pobratim!
Into grievous straits art thou come, unhappy one!
Yet do I swear by the faith of my body,   70
That I shall deliver thee, brother,
Be it by gold or by deed of prowess!"
He gat him up to his slender tower;
He sate him down for a space and drank his fill of wine,
Then he girded on his sabre well-forged,
He threw around him a cloak of wolf-skin,
On his head he set a cap of wolf-skin,
And bound it on with a brown head-cloth.
Then he took his battle-spear,
And descended to the stall of Sharatz.   80
He made ready his war-horse Sharatz,
He made fast the seven saddle-girths,
And bridled him with a gilded bridle.
He poured wine into the wine-skin,
And hanged it at the saddle-bow on the left hand,
On the right hand he hanged his heavy mace,
That the saddle might not slip this way nor that.
Then he threw himself on the back of Sharatz
And rode forth of Prilep town!
Towards Belgrade the capital he took his way[1],   90
And when he was come nigh to Belgrade,
He entered an inn and drank his fill of wine.
Then he laid a cloth over Sharatz[2],
And so came to the Danube ferry.
Twice Marko shouted for the ferryman,
Nor would wait for him no longer,
But urged Sharatz into the Danube;
Straight he went towards Varadin castle,
To the green meadows before Varadin.

[1] Оде право стојну Бијограду: "Straight he went to Belgrade the capital." стојни Биоград=Alba regia (Vuk).
[2] To conceal his identity.

There he halted the war-horse Sharatz,   100
He struck his spear into the untilled ground,
And tied Sharatz to the spear-shaft.
He unslung the wine-skin from the saddle-bow
And laid it on the green grass,
Then he sate him down and drank the dark wine.
He drank it not as men use to drink,
But he drank from a copper basin of twelve okas;
Half he drank, and half he gave to Sharatz.
When day dawned on the morrow,
Velimirovica was walking,—   110
The dear daughter-in-law of General Vuča—
On the wall of Varadin castle.
She looked downward to the green meadows,
She saw Marko in the meadow,
And when she saw Kraljević Marko,
An ague gat hold on her,
And she fled into the white manor.
General Vuča asked her:
"What aileth thee, dear daughter-in-law?"
Velimirovica answered him: 120
"Ah, father-in-law!
A knight sitteth in the wide meadow,
He hath planted his spear in the unploughed earth,
And hath tethered his horse to the spear-shaft,
And hard by there lieth a wine-skin:
He drinketh not as men use to drink,
But from a copper basin of twelve okas,
He drinketh half, and half he giveth to the horse.
His horse is not as other horses,
But brindled like as beeves;   130
The knight is not as other knights,
But on his shoulders is a cloak of wolf-skin,
On his head is a cap of wolf-skin
Bound on with a brown head-cloth;
In his teeth he holdeth something black,
That for size is as a lamb of half a year."

Vuča, the General, saith to her:
"Have no fear, dear daughter-in-law!
I have his fellows in the dungeon,
And him also I shall take presently."   140
He called to him his son Velimir:
"Velimir, my dear child!
Take three hundred horsemen, my son;
Go thou down to the wide meadow,
And bring me in yonder knight."
Velimir leapt to his feet,
He took three hundred horsemen;
He mounted his fiery black steed,
He rode out through the castle gate,
And compassed about Marko on four sides.   150
And ever Marko sat drinking the dark wine,
But Sharatz espied the horsemen,
He stamped on the ground with his hoofs,
And drew nigh to his master.
But anon when Kraljević Marko looked up
The horsemen already compassed him about.
Right so Marko drank a vessel of wine,
And threw the vessel down on the green grass;
Then he flung him on the back of Sharatz,
And with that the horsemen ran in upon him.   160
Had one but been there to see,
When Marko strake upon the horsemen,
Like a falcon among doves!
How many he slew with his rich-wrought sabre!
How many he trampled down beneath the feet of Sharatz!
How many he drowned in the silent Danube[1]!
The stripling Velimir fled before him,
Marko followed hard after him on Sharatz,
And overtook him in the wide meadow.
He smote him lightly with his mace,   170
The stripling fell down on the green grass.

---

[1] у тихом Дунаву: see note on тих in "A Damsel outwits Marko."
Here "quiet" or "smooth-flowing."

Marko lighted down from his horse Sharatz,
He bound the youth feet and hands,
And fastened him to the saddle-bow of Sharatz.
Then he hied him back to his wine-skin,
He cast the stripling down on the green grass,
And sate him down again for to drink wine.
All this Velimirovica perceived,
And she ran to General Vuča:
"A curse on thy wine, Vuča!   180
A curse on thy wine—and a double curse on thyself!
All thy horsemen have perished,
The knight hath bound Velimir's hands,
He hath bound his feet and his hands,
And behold he drinketh red wine,
And Velimir lieth on the sward!"
Vuča made answer:
"Be not adread, dear daughter-in-law,
Thou wilt see now—when the old man goeth forth!"
He caused the castle guns to thunder,   190
He assembled three thousand horsemen,
He mounted his Arab mare,
And rode out through the castle gate.
Down in the meadow he disposed the horsemen,
And from four sides they closed in.
Marko saw naught thereof,
But the war-horse Sharatz saw it;
He stamped on the ground with his hoofs,
And drew nigh to his master.
But anon when Kraljević Marko looked up,   200
The horsemen already encompassed him about!
Therewithal he sprang to his light feet,
And threw him on the back of Sharatz.
Ah, that one had been there to see,
How he drave the horsemen across the meadow!
His sabre was in his right hand,
In his left his battle-spear,
In his teeth the bridle;

Whomsoever Marko smote with his sabre
Was made two instead of one!   210
Whomsoever Marko smote with his spear,
Him he cast over his head!
And when he had turned him about once and again,
The troop of horsemen went to the devil!
Vuča fled from before him,
On his slender Arab mare,
Marko pursued after him on Sharatz.
Swift was the wild Arab of Vuča
And fain would Vuča take refuge in Varadin castle,
But Marko swung his heavy mace,   220
He hurled it after him athwart the fields,
And smote him with the mace handle.
Vuča fell down on the green grass;
Then Marko of Prilep lighted down,
He bound Vuča's hands behind his back,
He bound his feet and his hands,
And hanged him at the saddle-bow of Sharatz.
He seized the slender Arab steed,
And went again to Velimir the son.
He bound them fast each to other,   230
And flung them across the Arab mare;
He tied the Arab mare to Sharatz,
And hied him straightway to white Prilep,
And cast the twain into the dungeon.
Right so Vuča's wife wrote a letter,
And sent it to white Prilep:
"Brother-in-God, Kraljević Marko!
Slay not my Vuča,
Nor yet my son Velimir.
Ask, Marko, whatsoever thou wilt!"   240
The letter came to Kraljević Marko;
When he perceived what the letter told him,
Marko wrote another letter:
"Thou faithful wife of Vuča!
Do thou set free my three pobratims,

And give them three tovars of gold:
Set free also old Toplica[1],
And give him three tovars of gold[2],
For much time hath that knight lost yonder:
And give me three tovars of gold,   250
Because I have laid much labour on my Sharatz.
And if there be aught else, Lady,
Thou hast there Miloš of Pocerje,
Thou mayst accord thee with him."
The letter went to Varadin castle.
When it came to the General's wife,
She read the letter,
And sent the gold to Marko of Prilep;
Then she took the keys of the dungeon,
And opened the accursed dungeon,   260
And let out the three young Vojvodas,
And with them the aged Toplica;
She led them to the white tower,
And she let call skilful barbers;
The first washed, the second shaved them,
And the third cut their nails.
She brought them wine and rakia,
And fine meats of every sort.
She told them what Marko had done,
And to Vojvoda Miloš she said: 270
"Brother-in-God, Vojvoda Miloš,
Set free my lord,
And my son Velimir!"
Miloš of Pocerje answered her:
"Lady, have no fear,
Give me Vuča's black horse

[1] И пусти ми старога Топлицу. "Old Toplica" is here referred
to for the first time. In a footnote, however, Vuk remarks that there is
a variant which says that the father of Toplica Milan was imprisoned
in Varadin. In order to set him free the three heroes broke into the
stronghold but were themselves seized by Vuča.

[2] Tovar = the load carried by a pack-horse. I have sometimes translated this word by "a charge."

Which he rideth once in the year
When he goeth to church at Tekija[1],
That I may ride worshipfully across Njemadija[2];
And give me the golden carriage   280
With twelve black horses harnessed thereto,
Even as Vuča is wont to harness them,
When he goeth to the Kaiser of Vienna,
That it may carry the aged Toplica;
Give me the garments of Vuča
Which he weareth at Easter,
That I may clothe my Toplica."
Vuča's wife gave him all his request,
And to each a thousand ducats   289
For the wine that they should drink on the way to Prilep.
Then they departed unto white Prilep,
And right fair welcome they had of Marko;
Forthwithal he set free Vuča,
And his son Velimir also,
And gave him a great fellowship
For to ride with him to his castle at Varadin
And the Vojvodas divided the gold,
They drank red wine and were merry,
They kissed each other on the cheek;
Then each kissed the white hand of Marko,   300
And so they returned every each to his own manor.

[1] "Tekija is a little church between Varadin and Karlovac. I wrote down this poem as recited by Podrugović, but whether he knew about Tekija before or merely inserted the name here I do not know" (Vuk's footnote).

[2] Да поиграм преко Њемадије: "that I may prance across Njemadija." Njemadija: the location of this district has not been identified; the word may possibly signify "barren land."

MARKO KRALJEVIĆ AND THE FALCON

Marko Kraljević fell sick
   By the roadside, by the way of heroes,
Beside his head he thrust in his spear,
And to his spear he tethered Sharatz.
And thus spake Kraljević Marko:
"If one should give me water to drink,
If one should make a shade for me,
Such an one would win a place for his soul[1]."
Thither sped a falcon—that grey bird—
In his beak he carried water to him,   10
And gave to Marko water to drink.
He spread out his wings over Marko,
And so he contrived shade for Marko;
And Kraljević Marko said:
"O falcon, grey bird of mine,
What service have I done thee ever,
That thou shouldst give me water to drink,
And shouldst contrive a shade for me?"
The falcon bird made answer:
"Jest not, Kraljević Marko!   20
When we were in Kossovo battle,
And endured fierce onslaught of the Turks,
The Turks took me,
And clipped both my wings,
Then thou tookest me in, Marko,
And didst set me on a green fir-tree,
That the Turkish horses might not destroy me.
Thou gavest me the flesh of heroes to eat,
And red blood thou gavest me to drink,
'Twas then, O Marko, that thou didest me service!" 30

[1] *I.e.* a place in heaven.

MARKO KRALJEVIĆ AND THE FALCON
(Variant)

MARKO lay beside the Sultan's highway,
He wrapped him about in a green dolman,
He covered his face with a silver-worked kerchief,
He struck his spear into the ground upright,
And to the spear-shaft he tethered Sharatz.
On the spear sat an eagle—that grey bird—
He spread his wings, he made shade for Marko,
And in his beak he bare cold water
And gave to the wounded hero to drink.
Then from the woody hill the Vila called: 10
"God keep us—thou grey eagle-bird!
What kindness hath he showed thee ever,
Hath Marko Kraljević showed thee ever,
That thou spreadest thy wings to make a shade for him,
That in thy beak thou bearest cold water
And givest to the wounded hero to drink?"
But the eagle, that grey bird, made answer:
"Hold thy peace, Vila, be thou stricken dumb!
What hath he not done for me?
What hath not Marko Kraljević done for me? 20
Thereof shalt thou well wit and know.
When the army perished at Kossovo,
And both Emperors were slain,
Even Knez Lazar and Sultan Murad,
The blood that fell reached to the horses' stirrups,
Yea, and to the silken girdles of the knights,
That horses and knights swam therein,
Horse against horse, hero against hero!
And we birds flew thither anhungered,
Anhungered and athirst we flew, 30
We did eat of the flesh of heroes
And of the blood of heroes we did drink;

Anon my wings grew wet with blood,
The sun shined down from a clear sky withal,
And my wings waxed stiff,
That with my wings I might not fly.
But my companions flew thence,
And I remained in the midst of the level plain,
And the horses and the heroes trampled me under foot!
But God brought Kraljević Marko thither,   40
He took me from the blood of heroes,
And set me beside him on Sharatz;
He bore me to the greenwood,
And set me upon a fir branch.
From the skies there fell a slender rain
And my wings were cleansed,
That with my wings I might fly,
Yea, fly over the greenwood
For to join me with my fellows.
Yet another kindness he showed me,   50
Marko Kraljević showed me another kindness,
Thereof shalt thou well wit and know.
When the town on Kossovo plain went up in flames,
And in flames went up the tower of Hadji Aga,
My eaglets were there;
Marko Kraljević gathered them together,
He gathered them in his silken bosom
And bore them to his white manor.
He fed them a full month of days,
A full month and a week of days;   60
He set them free in the greenwood,
And I found my eaglets once again.
Thus did Marko for my sake!"
And men think of Kraljević Marko,
As of a lucky day in the year.

THE MARRIAGE OF MARKO KRALJEVIĆ

MARKO sat at supper with his mother,
  And she began to speak with Marko:
"O my son, Kraljević Marko,
Thy mother is now well stricken in years,
She cannot prepare thy supper,
She cannot serve the dark wine,
She cannot make light with the pine splinter.
Take thee a wife, therefore, my dearest son,
That so I may have a successor afore I die."
Marko said to his aged mother: 10
"God be my witness, dear old mother!
Through nine kingdoms have I been,
Yea, through ten, and the tenth was the Turkish Empire;
When I found a maiden for myself,
There was no friend for thee,
And when I found friends for thee,
For me there was no maiden there.
Yet stay, one maid there was,
At the court of King Šišman[1],
Mother mine, on Bulgarian soil,   20
I found her by the waters of the cistern,
And when I saw her, mother,
Meseemed the ground turned about me.
Behold, mother, the maid for me,
And for thee also worthy friends.
Make ready of slender meal-cakes,
That I may go and ask the maid in marriage."
Of that word had his mother exceeding great joy.
She waited not until the day dawned,
But already she made for him the sugared cakes.   30
And when day dawned on the morrow,
Marko made ready himself and Sharatz.

[1] Šišman = Sigismund.

He poured wine into a wine-skin,
He hanged it on the saddle of Sharatz,
And on the other side his heavy mace.
Then he mounted his fiery steed,
And went straightway to the Bulgarian land,
To the white palace of King Šišman.
From afar the King espied him,
And came out for to meet him.   40
They opened their arms and kissed each other on the face.
Each asked how it did with other.
The faithful servants took the horses,
And led them away to the stables below.
The King took Marko to the white tower,
They sate them down at the well-spread table,
And began to drink dark wine.
And when they had well drunken,
Marko sprang to his light feet,
He doffed his cap, he bowed him to the ground,   50
And asked the King to give him the maid in marriage.
The King gave her without a word,
And when Marko had gotten ring and apple[1],
And rich garments for the bride,
And had given gifts to mother-in-law and sister-in-law,
Marko had spended three tovars[2] of gold.
He required him respite for a month of days,
That he might fare to white Prilep
And gather the well-beseen wedding-guests.
The maid's mother said to him: 60
"O son-in-law, Marko of Prilep,
Bring not a dever[3] that is a stranger,
But either a brother or else a cousin,
For the damsel is peerless of beauty,
And we fear some deed of shame."

[1] The usual offering of a suitor. See "A Damsel outwits Marko."
The apple and quince are ancient symbols of fertility.
[2] The load carried by a pack-horse.
[3] Dever = bride-leader, best-man.

Marko tarried yet one night there.
In the morning he made ready Sharatz,
And hied him straightway to white Prilep.
When he drew nigh to Prilep castle,
From afar his mother espied him,   70
And came forth to meet him.
She opened her arms and kissed him on the face,
Marko kissed the white hand of his mother.
His mother asked Kraljević Marko:
"O my son, Kraljević Marko,
Hast thou journeyed in peace?
Hast thou won for me a daughter-in-law,
For me a daughter-in-law, for thyself a faithful wife?"
To his aged mother Marko made answer:
"Yea, mother, in peace have I journeyed,   80
I have wooed and won the maiden,
I have spent also three tovars of gold.
And when I left the white palace,
The maid's mother said to me:
'O son-in-law, Kraljević Marko,
Bring not as dever one that is a stranger,
But bring a brother or a cousin,
For the damsel is peerless of beauty,
And of some great shame we are adread!'—
And, mother, I have no brother,   90
I have no brother, nor no cousin."
The aged mother said to him:
"O my son, Marko of Prilep,
Have no care concerning that,
But do thou write a letter
And send it to the Doge of Venice.
Let him come as kum to the wedding,
Let him bring five hundred guests with him.
And do thou send another letter to Stepan Zemljić,
That he may be dever to the damsel.   100
Let him bring five hundred guests with him,
And so thou shalt fear no deed of shame."

When Marko heard these words,
He obeyed his mother.
He wrote the letters on his knees.
One he sent to the Doge of Venice,
The other to his pobratim, Stepan Zemljić.
And within a while,
Behold, the Doge of Venice,
With five hundred wedding-guests with him.   110
The Doge gat him to the slender tower,
And the guests encamped on the wide plain.
And within a while behold Stepan also,
With five hundred wedding-guests with him.
They met together in the slender tower,
And drank their fill of dark wine.
The wedding-guests departed thence,
And to the land of the Bulgars they went,
Straight to King Šišman's palace.
The King gave them fair welcome and according,   120
The horses were led to the cellars[1] below,
And the knights to the white castle.
He kept them for three white days,
The horses and the knights reposed them.
But when the fourth morning dawned,
The well-beseen čaušes cried:
"Up, ye wedding-guests, well-beseen!
Short are the days and long the stages,
Let us think of the homeward journey."
The King brought forth lordly presents.   130
To one he gave embroidered kerchiefs, to another apparel.
To the kum he gave a golden table,
To the dever a gold-embroidered shirt.
To the dever also he gave over the maid on horseback,
And to the dever thus spake the King:
"Behold, horse and maiden are in thy keeping,

[1] подрум = a cellar. The word, however, might be better rendered as "stable." Horses and cattle were lodged below the living-rooms, but not in a cellar in the underground sense.

As far as Marko's white manor.
There thou shalt give the fair maid to Marko,
The charger will be thy guerdon."
The well-beseen wedding-guests departed,   140
And took their way across the Bulgarian fields.
But where good fortune is—there also is evil fortune.
The wind blew on the wide plain,
And lifted the damsel's veil,
That the damsel's face was discovered.
The Doge of Venice saw her face,
And his head was filled with aching desire.
Scarce might he wait until night should come.
And when the wedding-guests had pitched their camp,
Then the Doge of Venice hied him   150
To the tent of Stepan Zemljić.
Softly he spake to Stepan:
"Dever," quoth he, "Stepan Zemljić!
Give me thy dear ward
To be my true love for one night.
See, here is a boot for thee full of gold,
Of yellow ducats, my Stepan."
Answered him Stepan Zemljić:
"Hold thy peace, Doge, mayst thou be changed into stone!
Art thou minded to perish?"   160
The Doge of Venice departed thence,
But when they were come to the next camping place,
The Doge hied him to the white tent,
And to Stepan Zemljić he said:
"Give me, Stepan, thy dear ward
To be my true love for one night.
Lo, here are two boots full of gold,
Of yellow ducats, my Stepan."
Stepan answered him bitterly:
"Get thee hence, Doge, mayst thou lose thy head!   170
How should she lie in the arms of her godfather?"
And the Doge returned to his tent.
But when they were come to the third camping place,

The Doge hied him to the dever Stepan:
"Dever," quoth he, "give me thy dear ward
To be my true love for one night.
See, here are three boots full of ducats for thee."
And Stepan Zemljić was corrupted
For three boots of yellow ducats.
He gave the Doge his dear ward,   180
He took from him three boots full of ducats.
The Doge took his god-daughter by the white hand,
He led her to his tent,
And spake smoothly to her:
"Sit thee down, my dear god-daughter,
That we may embrace and love each the other."
But the Bulgarian damsel answered and said:
"Unhappy godfather, Doge of Venice!
The earth would open under us,
The heavens would break above us.   190
How should thy god-daughter lie in thine arms?"
The Doge of Venice made answer:
"Speak not foolishness—dear god-daughter,
Already I have loved nine,
Nine god-daughters by baptism,
And twenty-four by marriage;
Nor once has the earth opened,
Nor the heavens broken above us.
Sit thee down that we may caress each the other."
But the maid said to the Doge: 200
"Godfather, Doge of Venice,
My old mother hath adjured me
Never to love a full-bearded hero,
But only a knight smooth of chin
Such as is Marko Kraljević."
When the Doge of Venice heard it,
He let come skilful barbers.
One washed him, the other shaved off his beard.
The fair damsel stooped down,
She gathered up the beard and wrapped it in a kerchief.   210

Then the Doge dismissed the barbers,
And spake softly to his god-daughter:
"Sit thee down, dear daughter."
But the Bulgar maid answered him:
"Ah, godfather, Doge of Venice,
If Kraljević Marko hear of this,
We shall both lose our heads."
The Doge said to the fair maiden:
"Sit thee down and play not the fool,
Marko is over yonder in the midst of the wedding-guests, 220
Where his white tent is pitched.
On the tent is a golden apple,
In the apple are two precious stones,
Which illumine half the camp,
So sit thee down that we may caress each the other."
The fair maid said to him:
"Wait yet a little, most dear godfather,
Until I go out before thy white tent
For to look at the sky,
Whether it be clear or cloudy." 230
And when she was gone out before the tent,
The maid perceived the tent of Kraljević Marko,
And lightly she leapt past the wedding-guests,
Like a roedeer a twelvemonth old,
To the tent of Kraljević Marko.
Within the tent Marko lay sleeping,
The maiden stood over him,
And down her fair face the tears ran.
Marko awoke and looked and was astonied,
Then to the Bulgar maid he said: 240
"Ignoble maid!
Mayst thou not endure
Until we come to my white manor,
And until the Christian law is accomplished?"
He seized his rich-wrought sabre,
But the fair damsel made obeisance,
And said to Kraljević Marko:

"Lord and master, Kraljević Marko,
I am not of ignoble stock,
But of a kingly line. 250
It is thou that leadest ignoble ones in thy train.
An ignoble kum, an ignoble dever.
Stepan Zemljić hath sold me
To the Doge, my godfather, for three boots full of gold.
And if thou believest me not, Marko,
See, here is the beard of the Doge of Venice."
And she shook the beard from out the kerchief.
When Marko Kraljević saw it,
He said to the damsel:
"Sit thee down, fair maid, 260
On the morrow Marko will seek them out."
And again he laid him down to sleep.
When day dawned and the sun cast his rays abroad,
Marko rose to his swift feet,
And donned his fur mantle with the hair outside.
In his hand he took his heavy mace.
Forthwith to the kum he went and to the dever,
And gave them fair good-morrow.
"Good-morrow," quoth he, "kum and dever!
And dever, where is thy ward? 270
Kum, where thy daughter?"
The dever held his peace—he said no word,
But the Doge of Venice answered:
"Marko Kraljević, my friend,
Folk are of strange humour nowadays,
One may not even jest in peace."
Said Marko Kraljević:
"An ill jest for thee, Doge of Venice!
No jest it was to shave off thy beard.
Where is thy beard of yesterday?" 280
The Doge would have answered him again,
But Kraljević Marko waited not.
He swung his sabre and cut off his head.
Stepan Zemljić fled,

[69]

But Kraljević Marko overtook him,
And smote him with the sword,
So that of one man he made two.
Then he returned back to his tent,
He made ready himself and Sharatz,
The well-beseen wedding-guests set out,   290
And in peace they journeyed to white Prilep.

MARKO KRALJEVIĆ RECOGNISES HIS FATHER'S SWORD

A Turkish damsel arose early,
   Before the dawning and the white day,
For to wash linen in the Marica river.
Before sunrise the water was clear,
After sunrise the water waxed dim.
And first with mud and blood it flowed,
Then it bare down horses and kalpaks,
And towards noonday wounded heroes:
And it bare with it a seemly knight,
The water took him in its current,   10
He rolled over and over down the Marica river.
The good knight perceived the damsel by the river,
And began to adjure her in the name of God:
"Sister-in-God, fair damsel!
Throw me an end of linen cloth,
Draw me out of Marica river
And I shall reward thee richly."
The damsel hearkened to him in God's name,
She threw him an end of linen,
And drew him out of the water to the bank.   20
Seventeen wounds had the knight,
And he wore gorgeous apparel.
On his thigh he bore a rich-wrought sabre,
On the sabre were three golden hilts,
On the hilts three precious stones;
And the sabre was worth three of the Sultan's cities.
The knight spake to the Turkish damsel:
"Sister mine," quoth he, "thou Turkish maiden,
Whom hast thou in thy white manor?"
Answered to him the Turkish damsel: 30
"I have an aged mother,
And I have a brother, Mustapha-Aga."
Then said the wounded knight:

"My sister—thou Turkish damsel,
Go, tell thy brother Mustapha-Aga,
That he may bear me to the white manor.
I have with me three purses of gold,
In each are three hundred ducats,
I shall give one to thee,
The second to thy brother, Mustapha-Aga,   40
The third I shall keep for myself
That I may heal me of my grievous wounds;
And if God will that I heal me of my wounds,
I shall give great recompense to thee;
To thee, and to thy brother Mustapha-Aga."
The damsel went to the white manor
And told her brother Mustapha-Aga:
"O brother, Mustapha-Aga,
I have found a wounded knight,
In Marica, in the cold river: 50
He hath on him three purses of gold,
In each are three hundred ducats;
One will he give to me,
The second will he give to thee, Mustapha-Aga,
The third will he keep for himself
That he may heal him of his grievous wounds:
Be not evilly advised
To slay the wounded knight,
But do thou bear him here to the white manor."
The Turk gat him to the river Marica,   60
And when he saw the wounded knight,
He began to examine the rich-wrought sabre.
On a sudden he smote with it and cut off the knight's head.
He stripped him of his rich apparel,
And returned back to the white manor.
His sister came out to meet him,
And when she saw what he had done,
She said to Mustapha-Aga, her brother:
"Wherefore hast thou done this, brother? May God
    do so unto thee!

Wherefore hast thou slain my pobratim? 70
For what hast thou done this evil?
For a rich-wrought sabre?
God grant it may cut off thine own head!"
Thus she said and fled into the manor.
Thereafter, but a short time had sped
When a firman came from the Turkish Sultan,
Laying charge on Mustapha that he should join the host,
So Mustapha joined him to the Sultan's host.
He had girded on the rich-wrought sabre
And when he came to the Sultan's host, 80
Great and small examined the sabre,
But none might draw it from its scabbard.
The sabre went from hand to hand,
It came into the hands of Marko Kraljević,
And for him the sabre left the scabbard of its own accord.
When Marko examined the sabre,
Lo, thereon were three Christian words!
The first was the name of Novak, the smith,
The second was the name of Vukašin the King,
The third was the name of Kraljević Marko! 90
Marko asked the Turk, Mustapha-Aga:
"Body of me, thou youthful Turk!
Whence hast thou this sharp sabre?
Hast thou bought it for gold?
Or hast thou won it in battle?
Was it bequeathed thee by thy father?
Or did thy wife bring it thee?
Did thy wife bring it as dowry?"
Mustapha-Aga, the Turk, answered him:
"Body of me, Giaour Marko! 100
Since thou askest, I will tell thee truly."
And he told him all even as it had come to pass.
To him spake Kraljević Marko:
"God do so unto thee, Turk, and more also!
Wherefore didst thou not heal his wounds?
I should have caused thee to receive favour

At the hands of our illustrious Sultan."
But Mustapha the Turk answered him:
"Go to, mock thou not, Giaour Marko!
If thou couldst in sooth command favour,   110
Thou wouldst grasp it for thyself first.
So give back to me the rich-wrought sabre."
Marko of Prilep swung the sabre
And strake off the head of Mustapha-Aga!
And there went that told it to the Sultan,
And the Sultan sent servants for Marko,
And every each as he came
Called aloud on Marko, but Marko answered not.
He abode where he sat, nor ceased from his wine.
And when it wearied Marko of the servants,   120
He donned his wolf-cloak of hide reversed,
He took his heavy mace,
And went and entered into the Sultan's tent.
So fierce within him was Marko's anger,
That booted[1] as he was he sate him down on the carpet,
He looked sideways at the Sultan,
And tears of blood stood in his eyes.
Now when the Sultan was ware of Marko,
That he had with him his heavy mace,
The Sultan went backwards and Marko followed after, 130
Until he drave him even to the wall.
Right so the Sultan put hand in pocket
And drew forth an hundred ducats,
And gave them to Kraljević Marko.
"Go, Marko," quoth he, "drink thy fill of wine.
What hath so sorely angered thee?"
"Ask me not, Sultan, my adopted father!
I have found my father's sabre.
If God himself had given it into *thy* hands,
I had been as wroth, every whit, with thee."   140
He arose and gat him to his tent.

---

[1] A studied insult on the part of Marko.

MARKO KRALJEVIĆ RECOGNISES HIS FATHER'S SWORD

(Variant)

THE Sultan's Majesty came down to Kossovo,
  With an hundred thousand warriors with him,
And camped by Sitnica river.
And a public crier[1] went through the host,
Offering for sale a damascened sabre.
The naked sword—three hundred ducats;
The sheath thereof—three hundred ducats;
Straps and swordbelt—three hundred ducats;
But none might he find
That would buy the sabre for gold.   10
But by chance it fortuned,
That Marko met with the Turk, the merchant,
And Kraljević Marko said:
"O Turk, thou crier of merchandise!
Give me the damascened blade that I may see it."
The Turk gave it without a word,
Marko looked well at the damascened sabre,
And to the crier he said:
"I will give thee nine hundred,
Nine hundred ducats, all of yellow gold,   20
But hear me, thou crier!
Let us seek a secluded spot,
Let us withdraw us from here a little,
That so I may count out to thee all the yellow ducats.
It liketh me not here to ungird me,
And to do off my three belts of gold,
For here I owe much money to a Turk,
He would not suffer me to buy the sword."
The Turk had joy of these words,
So they went up by Sitnica river,   30

[1] телал = herald, messenger, one who cries articles for sale.

Under the white stone bridge.
And Kraljević Marko ungirded,
And did off his three belts of gold;
He spread out a green mantle,
And emptied thereon his three belts of gold.
The Turk fell to counting all the yellow ducats,
What time Marko looked well at the Damascus blade,
And lo, upon the blade three Christian words!
The first was the name of Saint Demetrius,
The second was the name of the holy archangel,   40
The third was the name of King Vukašin.
And when Kraljević Marko perceived it,
He put question to the Turkish merchant:
"O Turk, thou crier of merchandise,
By the one only God,
Whence hast thou this Damascus sabre?
Came it to thee from thy father?
Or did thy wife bring it in wedding portion?
Or didst thou win it in battle?"
The Turk made answer to Marko: 50
"Body of me, thou unknown knight!
I will tell thee soothly!
The sabre came not to me from my father,
Nor did my wife bring it in wedding portion.
But hearken, unknown knight!
On the battle-field did I win the sabre,
When the Serbian Empire perished,
And two emperors fell at Kossovo,
Sultan Murad and Tsar Lazar,
There won I the sabre.   60
While it was yet early I hied me to Sitnica,
That I might water my stout steed,
And as it fortuned,
I came on a green silken tent.
Within the tent there lay a wounded knight,
Grim of aspect he was—God strike him dead!
His moustache fell down on his breast,

He had wrapped himself in a green mantle,
And beside him was the Damascus sabre.
And when the wounded knight was ware of me,   70
He spake, calling me brother-in-God.
'Brother-in-God,' quoth he, 'unknown knight,
Cut not off my head,
For I am grievously wounded,
And right soon will my soul go from me.
Do thou wait but one half hour,
And bury me by Sitnica river.
Lo, I have three belts of gold about me,
And behold my sabre damascened,
The which is worth a thousand ducats,   80
And my silken tent also.'
But of him truly, would I take no gift.
I drew him forth—the wounded hero—
I seized the sabre and cut off his head;
Then I took him by the hand,
Likewise by the right foot,
And cast him into Sitnica river.
It was there I won marvellous great booty,
And there I won me this sabre."
When Kraljević Marko heard it,   90
He spake to the crier of merchandise:
"O Turk, may God do so unto thee and more also!
Him thou slewest was my own dear father,
My father, King Vukašin!
Hadst thou waited for his soul to pass,
Hadst thou buried him yonder,
I would have given thee better burial."
Right so he drew the damascened blade,
And strake off the Turk's head.
He took him by the hand,   100
And cast him into Sitnica river.
"Go, Turk," quoth he, "seek my father!"
Marko returned back to the Sultan's host
Bearing with him both gold and sabre.

The Turkish janissaries questioned him, saying:
"God aid thee, Kraljević Marko!
Whither is gone the merchant?"
And Marko answered the Turks:
"He hath fared further, Turkish janissaries.
He took my ducats and piastres,   110
And fared further for to trade by the sea coast."
But the Turks spake among themselves, saying:
"Woe to the Turk that tradeth with Marko!"

MARKO KRALJEVIĆ AND PHILIP
THE MAGYAR

THIRTY captains sat at wine together,
In white Karlovatz town.
Amongst them Philip the Magyar,
And beside him Vuk the Firedrake[1].
And when they had well drunken,
And were flown with wine,
The thirty captains boasted themselves
How many slaves each had taken,
How many heads each had smitten off.
And Philip the Magyar spake: 10
"Brothers—ye thirty captains,
Ye see white Karlovatz,
How there are thirty and three towers therein?
I have garnished each with a head,
Save only the tower on the bridge,
And that too I shall presently garnish
With the head of Kraljević Marko."
Thus spake Philip the Magyar,
For he thought that none heard him,
None that was a faithful friend to Marko.   20
But Vuk the Firedrake heard him,
Pobratim to Kraljević Marko.
Right so he sprang lightly to his feet,

---

[1] Змај-Деспот Вук: lit. "Dragon-despot Vuk." He is a well-
known hero in the folk-ballads, where he is often referred to as змај
огнени or "the firedrake." Cf. Krauss, *Sl. Volkforschungen,* p. 332:
"Tiernamen kommen bei den Südslaven ungemein häufig als Fami-
lien- und noch mehr als Personennamen vor. Am gewöhnlichsten sind
vuk (Wolf), zmaj (Schlange, Drache), selten kuna (Marder). Als
Toteme sind diese Tiere international. Der südslavische Bauer benennt
sein Kind mit einem solchen Namen, um ein frühzeitiges Sterben des
Kindes zu verhüten....Es kommt indessen auch eine Kombinierung
zweier Totemnamen vor, so vuk-zmaj, oder vuk-zmaj ognjeni
= Wolf-Feuerdrache." See Appendix, p. 180.

He seized paper and inkhorn,
And wrote a letter withal,
To Prilep the white town,
To Kraljević Marko his pobratim.
And thus saith Vuk to Marko:
"Hear me, my brother-in-God!
Thou hast an ill enemy at Karlovatz,   30
To wit, Philip the Magyar.
He hath sworn, brother,
That he will smite off thy head,
And garnish a white tower therewith.
Therefore, brother-in-God, keep thee well
Against false treason on the part of Philip."
And Vuk sent him the letter.
When the letter came to Marko,
And he saw what his brother wrote to him,
He leapt to his light feet,   40
And made him ready in his white manor.
He girded on his rich-wrought sabre,
He cast his wolf-skin cloak about him,
He descended down to the stable,
And made ready stout Sharatz.
He covered him with a grey bear-skin,
And bridled him with a bit of steel;
He hanged his heavy mace on him,
With a sword on either side,
And flung himself on the back of Sharatz.   50
On his own back he slung his war-spear,
And straight through Kossovo plain he fared,
From Pazar by rugged Vlaha Stara,
And descended to the country round about Valjevo.
Straight athwart Mačva plain he fared
Until he came to Mitrovica town.
And there Marko ferried the Sava.
Straight athwart the Syrmian plain he fared,
And when he came to Karlovatz town,
He went down through the new market-place   60

Until he came to Philip's dwelling.
He caused enter Sharatz into the marble courtyard
And rode up before the white manor;
But Philip was not within,
For he was gone to the hills on hunting,
And his wife, Andjelija, stood before Marko.
About her were four handmaidens
Upholding her sleeves and the hem of her garment.
And when Marko came thither,
He cried greeting to her: 70
"God aid thee, dear sister!
Is pobratim Philip within?"
But Philip's wife made answer:
"Get thee hence, starveling dervish[1],
Philip is no brother to such as thee!"
When Kraljević Marko heard that,
He smote her in the face with the palm of his hand.
Now a golden ring was on his hand,
And it did scathe upon her visage,
And put out three sound teeth from their place.   80
Then he took from her three rows of ducats[2],
And cast them into his silken pocket,
And said to the wife of Philip:
"Give greeting to Philip the Magyar
When he cometh down from the hills.
Let him come to the new tavern,
That we may drink red wine and be merry,
Not with my gold nor yet with his
But with thy golden necklace."
He turned about the fiery Sharatz   90
And went straightway to the new tavern.
He lighted down from Sharatz and tied him before the tavern,
Then he sate him down to drink red wine.
No long time, nay, but a short time thereafter,
Came Philip to his white manor.

[1] гола дервишино. Dervish is a word of contempt.
[2] A necklace composed of three rows of gold coins.

Andjelija his wife met him,
Adown her fair face tears rolled,
And in her hands she held a blood-stained kerchief.
Philip the Magyar asked her:
"What aileth thee, my faithful wife,   100
That thou sheddest down tears from thine eyes,
And holdest a bloody kerchief in thy hands?"
His wife went to him and said:
"Lord and master, Philip,
When thou wentest to the hills on hunting,
And I remained behind by the white manor,
The Devil brought a certain dervish,
He wore a cloak of wolf-skin,
His sabre was girded on above his cloak,
A war-spear he bore behind him on his shoulders, 110
And he rode a piebald horse.
The horse he urged before the white manor,
And thus he gave me greeting:
'God aid thee—my dear sister!
Is pobratim Philip within?'
But I would none of his greeting,
And thus did I answer him:
'Get thee hence—thou starveling dervish!
Philip is no brother to such as thee!'
Forthwith he urged his piebald steed   120
And smote me on the face with the palm of his hand.
On his hand was a golden ring,
Sore scathe it did upon my fair visage,
And put out three sound teeth from their place.
He took from me the three rows of ducats,
And gat him forth to the new tavern.
And this greeting did he leave thee,
That thou shouldst get thee to the new tavern,
For to drink deep of the red wine,
Not with thy gold nor yet with his,   130
But with my golden necklace."
When Philip the Magyar heard it,

To his wife Andjelija he said:
"Peace, weep not, faithful wife!
Philip will straightway seize him,
And will bring him to the white manor,
To rock thy son in his cradle."
He turned his grey Arab mare about,
And forthwith went down through the market-place
Until he came before the new tavern.   140
But Sharatz was tethered by the door.
Philip urged his grey Arab mare,
For he would have her enter into the new tavern,
But the war-horse Sharatz suffered it not,
But with his hoofs smote her in the ribs.
Philip the Magyar waxed wroth,
He seized his studded mace
And made to smite Sharatz before the tavern;
But Sharatz lift up his voice in lamentation before the tavern:
"By the merciful God—woe is me!   150
That I should perish this morn before the tavern,
At the hands of mighty Philip the Magyar,
With my illustrious master nigh at hand!"
But from within Marko spake to him:
"Suffer him to pass, Sharatz!"
When Sharatz heard Marko,
He suffered him to pass into the new tavern.
And when Philip entered into the tavern,
He gave no "God aid thee,"
But grasped his heavy mace   160
And smote Kraljević Marko,
Smote him on his hero's shoulders.
Little enough recked Marko,
And to Philip the Magyar he said:
"Sit thee down in peace, thou Magyar bastard!
Wake not the fleas on my skin,
But light down from thy horse that we may drink wine.
There will still be time for fighting."
But Philip hearkened not unto Marko,

But he smote him on the right hand,   170
And brake his golden goblet,
And spilled out the red wine.
When Kraljević Marko saw it,
He leapt to his feat from the ground,
And made assault on the Magyar.
He seized his sabre,
And smote him with it,
He smote him on the right shoulder
And clave him in twain even on the saddle.
Through him went Marko's sword,   180
Even unto the door of marble stone,
And in twain it hewed him.
And when he had looked at the keen blade,
Quoth Marko:
"Dear God, a mighty marvel!
Good steel for an evil knight."
And he strake with it again and cut off his head.
Into Sharatz's corn-bag he flung the head,
And straightway went to Philip's dwelling.
Into the white treasure-chamber he went,   190
And took therefrom the treasure.
Then Marko went on his way singing,
But Philip lay in the throes of death[1],
And his young wife kept wailing.

---

[1] Оста Вилип ногом копајући: lit. "Philip remains digging the ground with his feet." This is a vivid picture of a man in his death-agony.

MARKO KRALJEVIĆ AND BEG KOSTADIN

Two pobratims rode their way together,
  Beg Kostadin and Kraljević Marko.
And Beg Kostadin said to Marko:
"Pobratim, Kraljević Marko,
An thou comest to me in autumn,
In autumn on Saint Demetrius' day,
On the day of my patron saint[1],
Thou shalt see brave festival,
And have brave welcome and according;
And lordly meats in goodly array."   10
Quoth Kraljević Marko:
"Boast not thyself, Beg, of thy hospitality,
Once when I sought my brother Andrea,
It fortuned I was in thy house,
In autumn, on Saint Demetrius' day,
On the day of thy patron saint.
I saw thy hospitality,
And I saw three unworthy deeds."
Quoth the Beg Kostadin:
"Pobratim, Kraljević Marko;   20
Of which unworthy deeds dost thou speak?"
Answered to him Kraljević Marko:
"This was the first unworthy deed, brother:
There came to thee two poor lads,
They asked of thee white bread to eat
And red wine to drink;
But thou saidst to the two needy ones—
'Get ye gone, vile outcasts,
Sully not my wine before these signors.'—
Sore grieved was I, Beg,   30
I was sore grieved for the two needy ones.
I took them both,

---

[1] Крсно име: another name for the Slava. See Appendix, p. 184.

I led them down to the market-place,
Of white bread I gave them to eat,
Of red wine I gave them to drink,
I let make for them garments of fine scarlet,
Of green silk and of fine scarlet.
And then I sent them to thy house.
As for me, Beg, I kept watch privily
How thou wouldest now receive them.   40
And thou tookest one of the needy ones,
Thou tookest him by the left hand,
The other thou tookest by the right hand,
Thou leddest them into thy house to the tables, saying:
'Eat and drink, young gentles,'—
And this, Beg, was the second unworthy deed:
There were present certain of ancient line
That had lost both goods and gear;
They were clothed in well-worn scarlet,
And to them thou gavest the lowest seats at the table.   50
And the upstart lords that were there,
That had but newly gotten goods and gear,
And wore new robes of scarlet,
Them didst thou set in the highest place;
Thou gavest them wine and rakia
And fine meats in goodly array.
The third unworthy deed, Beg, was this:
Thou hast both father and mother now living,
Yet not one nor other was at table,
For to drink the first glass of wine!"   60

MARKO KRALJEVIĆ AND ALIL-AGA

Two sworn brothers rode together
Through the fair city Tsarigrad.
The one was Kraljević Marko,
The other Kostadin Beg.
And Marko began to speak on this wise:
"Pobratim, Kostadin Beg,
Now that I go forth of Tsarigrad,
I might well meet with an errant knight
That should bid me have ado with him.
Therefore will I feign to be passing sore sick   10
Of the flux, an evil sickness and a terrible!"
So Marko feigned sickness,
Not being sick, but of his craftiness,
On stout Sharatz he bowed him down,
That he pressed on the saddle with his heart,
And so went forth of Tsarigrad.
And a worshipful adventure befell in the way!
There met him Alil-Aga, the Sultan's man,
With thirty janissaries with him,
And said Alil-Aga to Marko: 20
"Sir Knight, Kraljević Marko,
Come, let us prove whether of us hath more skill
    of bow and arrow,
And if God and fortune will well
That ye should outshoot me this day,
Then shall ye take my white manor,
And all the appurtenance thereof,
And the lady, my faithful wife.
But if I outshoot you this day,
I ask not your house not yet your wife,
But right so I will hang you,   30
And possess me of valiant Sharatz."
Kraljević Marko made answer:
"Leave me in peace, accursed Turk!

I assent not to this arrow-shooting,
For that a heavy sickness is upon me,
Even the flux, a sore sickness and a terrible!
Scarce may I hold me on horseback,
And how should I shoot with arrows?"
But the Turk would not depart from him,
But laid hold on the lappet of Marko's cloak on the
    right hand,   40
And Marko drew knife from girdle,
And cut off the right lappet of his mantle.
"Hence, villain," quoth Marko, "be ye accursed!"
But the Turk would not let be,
But laid hold on the left lappet of his cloak,
And Marko drew knife from girdle
And cut off the left lappet also:
"Hence, villain, God smite thee!"
But the Turk would not let be,
He laid hold on Sharatz by the bridle,   50
With his right hand he laid hold on the bridle of Sharatz,
With his left hand he seized Marko by the breast.
Then did Marko's wrath blaze forth like living fire;
Upright he sat on valiant Sharatz,
And drew in the reins to him,
That Sharatz danced as he had been mad,
And so sprang over horses and horsemen.
Then Marko called to him Kostadin Beg:
"Brother, Beg Kostadin," quoth he,
"Get thee to my house, brother,   60
Bring me thence a Tartar arrow,
In the which Tartar arrow
There be nine white falcon feathers:
As for me, I go with the Aga to the Kadi,
For to confirm our covenant in the tribunal,
That afterwards there be no strife betwixt us."
Then the Beg returned to the house
And Marko went with the Aga to the Kadi.
As he entered in, Alil-Aga, the Sultan's man,

Put off his shoon and sate him down by the Kadi.   70
He drew forth twelve ducats,
And set them under the knees of the Kadi.
"Effendi," saith he, "here be ducats,
Give not unto Marko a true judgment."
Now the Turkish tongue was understanded of Marko,
But he had no ducats,
So he set his mace across his knees
And, "Hearken to me," saith he, "Kadi-Effendi!
Give thou me true judgment,
For thou seest my gilded six-ribbed mace.   80
An I go for to smite thee therewith
No leech shall do thee none avail,
But thou shalt forget thy judgment seat
And nevermore shalt thou behold ducats!"
An ague gat hold on the Effendi
When he looked upon the golden-studded mace.
He gave true judgment and his hands shook.
Now when the heroes departed to the field,
With the Aga went thirty janissaries,
But there followed none after Marko,   90
Save only certain Greeks and Bulgars.
And when they were come to the field
Alil-Aga, the Sultan's man, saith to Marko:
"Fair Knight, come, loose thine arrows,
Thou vauntest thyself for a good knight of prowess,
Thou didst boast in the Sultan's Divan
How with an arrow thou mayst smite the eagle-bird[1],

---

[1] Ll. 97 and 98:

> Да застрелиш орла крстатога,
> Крсташ' орла, што води облаке.

> Thou shootest with an arrow the cruciform eagle,
> The cruciform eagle that leadeth the clouds.

This somewhat obscure reference to the "cruciform" eagle is supposed to mean that when the bird is soaring in the sky it bears to the
eye of a watcher on the ground a strong resemblance to a cross. It will
be remembered that the Vila is also credited with directing the clouds.
"The cloud-gatherer." See also the word ала in Vuk's *Dictionary*.

Even the eagle that leadeth the clouds!"
Kraljević Marko answered him again:
"Well I wot, Turk, I am a good knight of prowess   100
But here art thou preferred before me,
For here art thou in thine own domain,
And on the field thou hast preference before me,
For it is thou that hast challenged me.
Therefore, Turk, do thou first loose an arrow."
The Turk loosed a white arrow,
He loosed an arrow, they measured by ells,
And behold, he had sent the arrow an hundred and twenty.
Then did Marko loose his first white arrow
And sent it ells two hundred.   110
The Turk loosed his second white arrow,
Three hundred ells he sped it.
Marko loosed his second white arrow,
Five hundred ells he sped it.
The Turk loosed his third white arrow,
Six hundred ells he sped it.
Therewithal came Kostadin to Marko
Bearing the Tartar arrow,
In the which Tartar arrow
Were nine white falcon feathers.   120
Right so Marko loosed the Tartar arrow
And so it flew into the mist and stour,
That with the eyes none might follow it,
And how should his flight be meted?
Then the Turk wept and made great dole,
And began to beseech Marko:
"Brother-in-God, Kraljević Marko,
By the most high God and by Saint John,
And by thy fair religion,
Thou hast won upon me my white manor   130
And the lady, my faithful wife,
But hang me not, brother, I pray thee."
Quoth Kraljević Marko:
"O Turk, may the living God smite thee!

Thou callest me brother, and givest me thy wife!
But I have no need of thy wife,
For with us it is not like as with the Turks,
A brother's wife to us is as a sister.
In mine own house I have a faithful wife,
The lady Jelitsa—of noble stock.   140
And I would forgive thee all the despite thou hast done me,
Without thou hadst rent my cloak;
So do thou give me three charges of gold,
That I may let mend the lappets of my cloak."
The Turk skipped of joy and gladness,
He embraced Marko and kissed him,
And took him to his lordly manor.
For three white days he made him good cheer out of
      measure,
And gave him three charges of gold.
The lady, also, gave a gold-embroidered shirt,   150
And with the shirt a kerchief silver-wrought.
Also he gave him three hundred horsemen that should
      go with him,
That should go with him even to his lordly dwelling.
And ever from that day forth the days of their life,
They held the lands for the worshipful Sultan;
And wheresoever the enemies made mighty war on
      the land,
There Alil-Aga and Marko drave them back,
And wheresoever cities were taken,
Alil-Aga and Marko were at the taking.

MARKO KRALJEVIĆ AND MINA OF KOSTURA[1]

MARKO sat at supper with his mother,
They supped on dry bread and red wine.
And there came three letters to Marko;
One letter was from Constantinople,
From the Sultan Bajazet.
The second letter was from Buda town,
And it came from the king thereof.
The third letter was from Sibinj[2],
From the Vojvoda Janko of Sibinj.
In the letter from Constantinople,   10
The Sultan called him to his standard
In the harsh country of the Arabs[3].
As for the letter from Buda town,
The king asked him therein to his wedding,
For to be his wedding kum,
For he would wed with a Lady Queen.
In the letter from Sibinj
Janko prayed him to be a kum,
That he might christen his two little sons.
And Marko asked his old mother of counsel: 20
"Counsel me, mother," quoth he,
"Whither were I best to go?
Shall I go to the Sultan's army,
Shall I go to the king's wedding
For to wed him with his Lady Queen,

---

[1] The name of a town in Macedonia (Vuk, *Dict.*).

[2] Sibinj or Hermannstadt (Lat. Cibinium). Janko of Sibinj is the same as Hunyadi Janos.

[3] Арапин is a word of somewhat vague meaning. Vuk says it is equivalent to "Maurus" and "Aethiops." Dozon says it includes Arabs, Moors and negroes. He adds: "Il y a sans doute dans ces campagnes lointaines de Marko une réminiscence historique, car on assure que Bajazet, dans la bataille où il fut défait par Timour, en 1402, avait parmi ses troupes vingt mille auxiliaires serbes." *Poésies pop. serbes*, p. 122.

Or shall I go to Janko of Sibinj
That I may christen his two little sons?"
Marko's mother answered him:
"O my son, Kraljević Marko,
A man goeth to a wedding for to be merry,   30
He becometh kum because his faith bids him.
But to the army he goeth of necessity.
Go, my son, to the Sultan's army,
God will forgive us, my son,
The Turk would never forgive."
Marko hearkened unto his mother,
And made him ready to go to the Sultan's host;
And took his servant Goluban with him.
And as he went about to depart he warned his mother:
"Hearken unto me, O mother!   40
Shut the doors of the castle early,
And in the morning open them late,
For I am at feud, mother,
With the acccurséd Mina of Kostura,
And I am sore adread
That he will plunder my white manor."
Marko departed to the Sultan's army
With his servant Goluban;
And when they were come to the third halting place,
Marko sate him down to sup,   50
And Goluban served the red wine.
Kraljević Marko took the goblet,
He took it and fell in such a study
That he let fall the goblet on the table;
The goblet fell, but the wine spilled not.
Goluban his servant awaked him.
"Lord and master, Marko," quoth he,
"Oft hast thou been with the army,
But never hast thou drowsed in this wise,
Nor let fall the cup from thy hand."   60
Then Marko came forth of his study,
And spake to his servant Goluban:

"Goluban, my faithful servant,
A moment agone I dreamed a marvellous dream,
A strange dream in a strange hour!
A saw where a cloud of mist arose[1]
From the white castle of Kostura,
And it rolled together around Prilep.
In that mist was Mina of Kostura,
He plundered my white manor,   70
Everything he plundered and burnt with fire.
Mine old mother he trampled under horses' feet,
He took captive my faithful wife,
He took my horses from the stables,
And my gold from the treasure-chamber."
To him Goluban his servant made answer:
"Fear not, Kraljević Marko!
A good knight hath dreamed a good dream.
Dreams are but lies, God is truth."
And when they were come to Constantinople,   80
The Sultan moved his mighty host
And they put forth across the dark sea,
To the dread country of the Arabs.
And they took cities by the sea,
Four and fifty cities.
But when they came to Kara-Okan[2],
There they tarried three years of days.
By Okan they tarried, nor might they take it.
And Marko cut down the Arab knights,
And brought their heads before the Sultan,   90
And the Sultan gave gold therefor to Marko.
Now this was very grievous in the sight of the Turks,
And they spake to the illustrious Sultan, saying:
"Lord and master, Sultan Bajazet,
Marko is no such knight of prowess,
But he cutteth off the heads of the slain
And bringeth them before thee for recompense."

---

[1] Cf. Momčilo's dream in "The Marriage of King Vukašin."
[2] Kara-Okan has not been identified.

Marko Kraljević heard it,
And he prayed the illustrious Sultan:
"O Sultan, my lord and father,   100
Tomorrow is my Slava day,
The day of fair Saint George.
Give me leave, my father[1],
That I may hold my Slava
According to law and custom,
And give me my pobratim Alil-Aga,
That I may drink wine in peace."
The Sultan might not otherwise,
So he sent forth Kraljević Marko
That he should celebrate his Slava,   110
And he gave him his pobratim Alil-Aga.
Marko went into the greenwood
Afar from the Sultan's army;
He pitched his white tent,
He sat down under it and drank dark wine
With his pobratim Alil-Aga.
And at dayspring of the morn,
Forthwith the Arab posts were ware
That Marko was not with the host,
And they cried aloud, saying: 120
"Charge now, fierce Arabs,
For the terrible knight is departed
That rode on the great piebald steed!"
Then the fierce Arabs charged,
And warriors thirty thousand assailed the Sultan.
Right so the Sultan wrote a letter to Marko:
"Come quickly, Marko, my son,
Thirty thousand warriors assail me!"
And Marko made answer to the Sultan:
"With all speed, O my father, the Sultan!   130
But not yet have I drunk my fill of wine,
Nor am not near risen from my Slava."
And when the dayspring of the second morn was come,

---

[1] поочим.

Again the Arab watchers cried:
"Charge, fierce Arabs!
For departed is the terrible knight
That rideth on the great piebald steed."
Forthwithal the Arabs hurled forward,
And sixty thousand warriors assailed the Sultan.
Again the Sultan wrote a letter to Marko: 140
"Come quickly, my son Marko!
Sixty thousand warriors assail me!"
But Marko made answer to the Sultan:
"Wait yet a little, my father, the Sultan,
Not yet have I enough feasted
With my fellowship of kums and friends."
And at the dayspring of the third morn,
Again the Arab watchers cried:
"Charge, fierce Arabs!
Departed is the terrible knight   150
That rideth on the great piebald steed."
Forthwithal the Arabs hurled forward,
And an hundred thousand warriors assailed the Sultan.
Right so the Sultan sent to Marko a letter:
"See that thou come quickly, son Marko!
See that thou come quickly, Marko, my son-in-God.
The Arabs have overthrown my tent."
Then Marko mounted him on Sharatz,
And went and joined him to the Sultan's host.
In the morning when the white day dawned,   160
The Arab watchers espied him,
And they cried from out their white throats:
"Give back now, fierce Arabs!
Behold he cometh, the terrible knight
On the great piebald steed!"
Then Marko smote down among the Arabs,
And brake their host in three parts.
The first he hewed in pieces with the sword,
The second he trampled under foot of Sharatz,
And the third part he drave before the Sultan.   170

But Marko was full sore wounded;
Seventy wounds had he gotten,
From the Arabs he had gotten seventy wounds.
And he fell down across the Sultan's knees,
And the Lord Sultan asked him:
"My son, Kraljević Marko,
Are thy wounds to the death?
Thinkest thou to be made whole of thy wounds?
Shall I let bring salves and leeches?"
Kraljević Marko made answer: 180
"My Lord, my father the Sultan!
My wounds are not unto the death,
Meseemeth I should well amend me."
The Sultan put his hand in his pocket,
And gave him a thousand ducats,
And he went forth to let search his grievous wounds.
And he sent two faithful servants after Marko
Who should see that he died not.
But Marko went not to no leeches,
But he went from inn to inn   190
Seeking where should be the better wine.
Scarce had Marko drunken somewhat,
When his sore wounds healed and were abated.
Therewithal came a letter to him,
How that his manor was plundered,
Yea, plundered and burnt up with fire.
How that his old mother was trampled under of horses;
How that his faithful wife was taken captive.
Then did Marko make great dole and sorrow,
On his knees before his father the Sultan: 200
"Lord and master," said he, "my father the Sultan,
My white manor is plundered,
My faithful wife is made captive,
Mine old mother is trampled on of horses,
The gold is taken from my treasure-chamber,
Mina of Kostura hath taken it."
The Lord Sultan soothed him, saying:

"Fear not, my son Marko!
And if thy manor be burnt
I shall build thee yet fairer dwelling,   210
Hard by mine own, and like even unto mine.
If thy gold be taken,
I shall make thee collector of poll-tax,
Thence shalt thou glean more gold than ever tofore.
And if thy wife be in sooth led captive,
I shall wed thee to a better one."
But Marko Kraljević answered:
"Thanks be to thee, my father the Sultan!
But, and if thou build me a manor,
The poor will curse me, saying: 220
'See the whoreson Kraljević Marko!
His old manor is burnt with fire,
May his new one avail him naught!'—
And if thou make me collector of poll-tax,
I may not gather the taxes,
If I bind not the poor and needy.
And the poor will curse me—
'See the whoreson Kraljević Marko,
The gold he had was ravished away,
May this gold also do him naught of profit.'—   230
And wherefore shouldst thou wed me to another wife,
Since that mine own is yet on live?
But give me three hundred janissaries,
Let forge for them the crooked knives of the vineyard,
And furnish them with light mattocks,
And I shall go to white Kostura
If haply I may win back my wife."
The Sultan gave him three hundred janissaries,
He let forge the knives of the vineyard,
And gave them light mattocks withal.   240
Then Marko gave counsel unto the janissaries:
"My brothers, ye three hundred janissaries,
Ye must get you to white Kostura;
And when ye come to the castle of Kostura

The Greeks will rejoice, saying:
'God be praised, here be day-labourers a many,
And for small wages will they labour in the vineyard.'—
But ye will not so, dear brethren,
But ye will tarry by the castle of Kostura,
Wine ye will drink and clear rakia,   250
Till that I also be come to Kostura."
The three hundred janissaries went forth,
They went forth to white Kostura,
And Marko gat him to the far-famed Holy Mountain[1],
He took the Sacrament and confessed him,
For he had done many a deed of blood.
He did on a monk's raiment,
And let grow his black beard to his girdle,
And on his head he set the priestly kamilavka.
Then he sprang on the back of Sharatz   260
And straightway went to white Kostura.
When he came to Mina of Kostura,
Lo, Mina sat drinking wine,
And Marko's wife served him.
"Ha, black monk!" quoth he,
"Whence hast thou yonder piebald steed?"
Kraljević Marko made answer:
"Faith of me, Lord Mina!
I was aforetime with the Sultan's host
In the dread country of the Arabs,   270
And there was one of little wit[2]
Whose name was Kraljević Marko,
And there in good sooth he perished,
And I buried him,
According to law and custom,
And for his soul's weal he gave me the horse."
When Mina of Kostura heard it,
He leapt lightly to his feet for gladness,
And he said to Kraljević Marko:

[1] Mount Athos.
[2] једна будалина = a fool.

"Good tidings, i'faith, black monk!   280
Behold, I wait nine years of days
That I might hear such tidings,
I have plundered Marko's manor,
Yea, plundered it and burnt it with fire;
I have made captive his faithful wife,
But not yet have I wedded her,
But have waited ever for the death of Marko,
And now shalt thou wed me to her."
Kraljević Marko took the book,
The book he took and wedded Mina,   290
And to whom but to his own wife!
Then he sate him down and drank wine,
Wine he drank and made good cheer,
And Mina of Kostura spake and said:
"Hearken, Jela, my heart and my soul!
Till now hast thou been called Marko's,
From now thou art Lord Mina's lady.
Go down, my soul, to the treasure-chamber
And of ducats bring three goblets full,
That I may reward the black monk."   300
Jela went down to the treasure-chamber,
And of golden ducats she brought three goblets full.
But she fetched them not from Mina's treasure
But she fetched them forth of Marko's treasure.
And she brought his rusty sabre,
And gave it to the black monk, saying:
"Take this also, black monk,
For the soul's weal of Kraljević Marko."
Kraljević Marko took the sabre,
He took the sabre and examined it,   310
And he spake to Mina of Kostura:
"Wilt thou grant in this thy gladness
That the monk may tread a merry measure?"
Mina of Kostura made answer:
"I will well, thou black monk,
I will well, and wherefore should I not grant it?"

Marko leapt lightly to his feet,
He turned him about two times and three times,
And all the castle shook to its foundations.
Then he pulled out his rusty sabre,   320
From right to left he swung it,
And hewed off Mina's head!
Then he cried with a loud voice:
"Charge now, my labourers!
Mina of Kostura is no more!"
The three hundred janissaries hurled forward
Against the stronghold of Mina of Kostura.
They plundered his white manor,
They plundered it, yea, and burnt it with fire!
Marko took his faithful wife,   330
He took Mina's treasure also,
And went his ways to white Prilep,
Singing and ever singing.

MARKO KRALJEVIĆ AND THE
TWELVE MOORS

KRALJEVIĆ MARKO set up his pavilion
In the harsh country of the Moors.
He sate him down to drink wine in his pavilion,
But or ever he had drained the glass,
A slave-girl came and ran,
And entered into the tent of Kraljević Marko.
Therewithal she began to beseech Marko:
"Brother-in-God, Kraljević Marko,
By the most high God, and by Saint John,
Save me from the Moors this day.   10
For I am come into the hands of three,
And this day I go to the fourth
Of twelve Moorish brethren,
And they entreat me not as wont is,
But scourge me with a threefold scourge,
And constrain me to kiss them.
Unhappy that I am! I may not suffer to look upon them,
Far less to bestow upon them kisses!"
Marko took her by the hand,
He made her to sit down by his right knee,   20
And covered her with a figured mantle.
In her hand he set a glass of wine.
"There, damsel!" quoth he, "Drink thy fill,
This day hath the sun risen upon thee,
Since thou art come to me into my tent."
Scarce had the damsel taken the glass
And raised it up for to drink the wine,
When lo, the twelve Moors were come
On twelve Arab coursers.
And forthwithal they reviled Marko: 30
"Thou whore! Kraljević Marko,
Art thou become another ruler over the land,

That thou takest from Moors their slave-girls?"
Kraljević Marko laughed:
"Get ye hence," quoth he, "Moorish children,
That I lay no sin upon my soul because of you."
But the twelve Moors waxed wonderly wroth,
And every each of them drew sword,
And overthrew the tent upon Marko.
They cut through the tent ropes   40
That the tent fell down upon the falcon Marko,
And on his battle-flag that bare the rood,
And upon Sharatz his stout steed.
When Kraljević Marko perceived
That his silken tent was overturned
Marko's wrath blazed up like living fire.
Lightly he leapt to his feet,
And seized great Sharatz.
To horse he sprang behind the damsel,
Three times he girdled her with his girdle,   50
And the fourth with his sword-belt.
Then he pulled out his well-forged sword,
And so ran on the Moors.
Not to the white throat he carved them,
But he carved them even to the silken girdle;
One man became two,
Out of twelve Marko made twice so many,
Of twelve Moors he made four and twenty.
And so he passed athwart the level plain,
Like a star athwart a clear sky.   60
Straight to Prilep town he went
To his white manor.
He called Jevrosima his mother:
"Jevrosima," quoth he, "mine aged mother,
Mother, my sweet, dear one,
Behold, mother, my sister-in-God.
Nourish her, mother, as thou hast nourished me,
Give her in marriage as she were thine own daughter,
That in this wise we may gain friends."

[103]

Jevrosima, the matron, nourished her,   70
Yea, and gave her in marriage
In Rudnik the white town,
In the great house of Dizdarić
Where were nine fair brethren.
Thence had Marko strong friends,
And oft would he visit his sister-in-God,
As she had been his own born sister,
And there full oft he quaffed the wine-cup.

MARKO KRALJEVIĆ AND THE DAUGHTER
OF THE MOORISH KING

Marko's mother asked a question:
"Ah, my son, Kraljević Marko,
Wherefore dost thou build so many pious buildings?
Hast thou sinned greatly against God?
Or doth gold come to thee without labour[1]?"
Marko of Prilep answered her:
"I'faith, old mother mine,
Once that I was in the land of the Moors,
I arose early and went to the cistern
For to water my Sharatz.   10
And when I was come to the cistern,
Lo, twelve Moors were there.
And before my turn, mother,
I would have watered my Sharatz.
But the twelve Moors would not so,
And there was strife betwixt us.
I took my heavy mace,
And smote a black Moor,
I smote down one, and there smote me eleven;
I smote down two, and there smote me ten;   20
I smote down three, and there smote me nine;
I smote down four, and there smote me eight;
I smote down five, and there smote me seven;
I smote down six, and there smote me six;
And these six put me to the worse!
They bound my hands behind my back
And took me to the Moorish King.
The King cast me into the depths of a dungeon,
Where for seven years I languished.
I knew not when summer came,   30

---

[1] "Лудо благо задобио" значи: без муке и без памети. само срећом, а много блага. (Vuk's footnote.)

Nor knew I when came winter,
Save by one token, mother.
In winter the damsels as they played at snowballs,
Would throw to me a snowball,
By that I knew that winter was come.
In summer they would throw me a spray of basil,
By that I knew that it was summer.
When the eighth year began,
It was not the prison that tormented me,
But a Moorish maiden, 40
Dear daughter of the Moorish King.
Morning and evening she would come,
And call to me through the dungeon window:
'Pine not away, unhappy Marko, in thy dungeon!
But give me thy solemn oath
That thou wilt take me to wife,
And I shall deliver thee out of prison,
And thy good Sharatz out of his stable.
I shall take of yellow ducats,
My poor Marko, as many as thou pleasest.' 50
When I considered of my evil plight,
I took off my cap and laid it on my knee,
And swore to the cap on my knee, saying:
'I take solemn oath I will not leave thee,
I take solemn oath I will not deceive thee.
The sun himself breaketh faith,
And warmeth not the earth in winter as in summer,
But never will I break mine oath!'
The Moorish maiden pondered this,
Thinking it was to her I swore. 60
On a night when darkness was come,
She opened the door of my dungeon,
She led me forth of the dungeon, mother,
She brought me the fiery Sharatz,
And for herself a better still than Sharatz,
And on both were saddle-bags full of ducats.
She brought me my rich-wrought sabre.

We mounted our horses,
And departed thence through the land of the Moors.
On a morning, as day dawned,   70
I sate me down to rest,
And the Moorish maiden took me,
Encircling me with her black arms,
And when I looked on her, mother,
On her black face and white teeth,
A loathing gat hold on me;
I drew the rich-wrought sabre,
And smote her on the silken girdle,
That the sabre cut clean through her.
I mounted my Sharatz,   80
And the head of the Moorish girl spake and said:
'Brother-in-God, Kraljević Marko!
Leave me not! Leave me not!'
Therein, mother, I sinned against God,
Gaining much gold thereby,
And for this cause I let build many pious buildings."

MARKO IN THE DUNGEON OF AZAK

(Fragment)

Dear God, to thee be praise in all things!
  What a knight of worship and hardiness was Marko!
And see how he fareth this day in a dungeon,
The accursed dungeon of Azak!
The dungeon is a strange abode.
Therein the water came to his knees,
And the bones of dead heroes reached to his middle.
And there went to and fro snakes and scorpions;
The snakes sought men's eyes for to suck;
The scorpions sought faces for to mar them,   10
The legs of heroes were loosed from their knees,
And their arms fell from their shoulders.
In the dungeon Marko made dole and sorrow out of measure;
Such dole he made that God himself was ware of it.
And Marko looked out to the market-place of Azak,
If haply he might see one of his own men.
And by the one God, none of his own he saw,
But he saw a fair damsel,
The dear daughter of the King of Azak.
And he called unto her, saying: 20
"Sister-in-God, thou king's daughter!
Draw nigh to me to the window of the dungeon."
The damsel hearkened unto him for God's sake,
For the sake of her brother-in-God.
She came nigh to the dungeon window,
And Marko spake (softly) to her:
"Sister-in-God, king's daughter!
Go to thy father, King of Azak;
Give him fair reverence from me and greeting:
By the true God I beseech him   30
That he let me forth of the accursed dungeon.
On my faith and honour,

And the guaranty of the true God,
That I may go to Prilep castle,
And bring him gold for ransom.
Twenty charges of gold, by the faith of my body!
And if he will not believe me,
Let him bring me forth of the accursed dungeon,
Let him bind me in iron,
And I will send a letter   40
To my mother in Prilep castle,
And she will bring the gold for ransom,
For I may not long endure in the dungeon."
When the damsel understood his words,
She went to the Divan to the King.
And when she was entered into the Divan to her father,
The King of Azak asked her:
"Marry, my dear daughter!
What lackest thou now?
A little silk, perchance, or velvet?   50
Or gold, or haply white linen?
Or fine cloth of Paragun[1],
Cut and uncut?"
Answered him the fair damsel:
"O my father, King of Azak!
In thy palace there is enough and to spare,
Nor am I in lack of aught.
I bring thee reverence and greeting,
From the prisoner, Kraljević Marko.
He prays thee to let him forth of the dungeon, father,   60
On his faith and honour,
And on the guaranty of the true God,
Till he may go to Prilep castle,
And he will bring thee gold for ransom.
Twenty charges of gold he will bring thee:
But, and if thou wilt not believe him,
Let him nevertheless forth of the dungeon;

[1] In his glossary at the end of vol. II of the Народне Пјесме, Vuk
says he does not know what "cloth of Paragun" may be.

Let bind him with fetters of iron,
And he will send a letter
To his mother in Prilep castle,   70
And she will bring thee gold to his ransom."
When the King of Azak heard it,
He spake harsh words to the damsel:
"A bitch thou art and not my daughter!
Thou art become his leman bitch!
By the Almighty God,
I will not let Marko forth of the dungeon,
But will hold him nine years,
Till the snakes have sucked his eyes,
And the scorpions have marred his visage: 80
Until his legs fall from the knees,
And his arms from his shoulders.
When Marko has suffered these torments,
I shall let forth the captive, without ransom,
I shall turn him a cripple into the street.
Let him beg for bread to nourish him!"
When the damsel understood these words,
She went to Marko's dungeon
And told him all that the King had said.
When Kraljević Marko heard it,   90
He made such dole that even God was ware of it,
And to the damsel he said:
"Sister-in-God, king's daughter,
Bring me inkhorn and paper,
That I may prepare a letter,
And send it to my mother at Prilep,
That she may sell lands and cities.
Let her sell them, and give money for my soul,
And nourish her, and protect her from evil.
As for my faithful wife, let her wed with another.   100
Dear Sister, let them no longer swear by me!
For here my bones do rot
In the accursed dungeon of Azak."
She brought him inkhorn and paper,

And he prepared a letter,
But he sent it not whither he had told her,
But sent it across the dark sea,
Across the sea to Salonica city,
To Dojčilo, his pobratim-in-God:
"O Dojčilo, pobratim-in-God,   110
I am fallen on evil days,
And suffer torment at the hands of the Arabs;
Enslaved am I and in a dungeon,
In Azak, in an accursed dungeon,
And I may not long endure in the dungeon,
For me a dungeon is an unwonted lodging;
Deliver me if God thou knowest!"
Then he called to him his grey falcon[1]:
"O falcon, fail me not at thy peril!
Bear this letter to Salonica city,   120
To Dojčilo, my pobratim-in-God,
That he may deliver me out of this dungeon."
The falcon took the letter
And he soared to the sky.
Straight he went to Salonica city.
Now it was morn of the Sabbath day,
And the lords of Salonica were in church,
In the white church were the lords of Salonica,
At matins and at the liturgy.
The falcon came to the white church,   130
The falcon screamed that God himself heard it,
The Vojvoda Dojčilo knew it

[1] Ll. 118–136: cf. "The Gay Goshawk":
  And when he flew to that castle
  He lighted on the ash;
  And there he sat and sang their loves,
  As she came from the mass.
   * * * *
  She's gane unto her west window,
  And fainly aye it drew,
  And soon into her white silk lap
  The bird the letter threw.

And came forth of the white church,
And sate him down on a silver settle.
To him came the grey-green falcon
And let fall the letter from beneath his wing.
Dojčilo took the letter.
When he saw what the letter told him,
He smote his knee with his hand,
He split the new cloth on his knee   140
And the golden wedding-ring on his hand.
And tears ran down his cheeks:
"Alas, brother, Kraljević Marko!
Thou art indeed fallen on evil days;
Not lightly shalt thou be delivered."
Then he bethought him how and what he should do.
All ways he pondered and one way he chose.
He took black dye,
And dyed black his white face;
He made of himself a black Arab,   150
And he led out his good brown steed.
On the brown steed he went with speed,
And came forthwith to Azak town.
And when he was come to the plain of Azak,
Fiercely he spurred his steed;
The good horse reared and sprang,
Sideways he sprang twelve ells,
In breadth four and twenty,
In height three mighty spear-lengths.

MARKO AND THE MOOR

A BLACK Moor builded him a manor,
He builded a manor of twenty storeys,
By the wide blue sea.
And when the Moor had finished his manor,
He set glass in the windows thereof,
And spread therein silk and velvet,
And thus he spake to his manor:
"Wherefore shouldst thou be desolate on the sea-coast,
    O manor?
There be none to come and go about thee,
For I have no mother nor no sisters,   10
Nor have I yet married me;
But I swear my wife shall come and go about thee,
Else am I not the son of my mother,
But the offspring of an Arab mare.
I shall woo the Sultan's daughter,
And either he shall give her to me,
Or he shall come out into the field against me."
Thus spake the Arab to his manor,
And forthwithal he wrote a letter,
And sent it to Stamboul to the Sultan: 20
"Sire, Sultan of Stamboul!
By the sea I have builded a manor,
And none cometh and goeth about it,
For I have not yet married me,
Give me then thy daughter in marriage;
But if thou wilt not give her to me,
Come out into the field against me."
The letter came to the illustrious Sultan;
When he perceived what the letter told him,
He let seek knights of prowess,   30
And he promised gold out of measure
To whomsoever should slay the black Arab.
And there went forth hardy knights a many,

But not one returned to Stamboul.
In sore straits was the Sultan,
For his best knights were gone from him,
The black Arab had slain them all.
Nor was that thing the most grievous,
For now the black Arab made ready
To go forth from his white tower by the sea-shore.　40
He put on him fine raiment,
And girded on his rich-wrought sabre,
And made ready his grey Arab mare;
About her he made fast the sevenfold saddle-girth,
And bridled her with a gilded bridle;
He made fast his tent to the saddle-bag on one side,
And on the other side he hanged his heavy mace;
He flung him upon his horse's back,
And slung his battle-spear behind him,
And straightway went to white Stamboul.　50
When he was come before the gate of Stamboul,
He struck his spear into the ground before the gate,
And to the spear he tied his Arab steed.
Then he pitched his white tent,
And on Stamboul he laid a tax
That each night they should give him a barren sheep,
A baking of white bread,
A cask of strong rakia,
Two casks of red wine,
And a fair damsel.　60
And she served him with red wine,
And at night he kissed her fair face.
And each day he sent a damsel to the land of Talia,
And thereby gained gold out of measure.
And so for three months he continued.
And a greater shame the Sultan suffered,
For the Moor bridled his slender mare,
Through white Stamboul city he urged her,
And went straightway to the Sultan's palace.
With a loud voice he hailed the Sultan:　70

"Ho, Sultan, bring forth thy daughter:"
Right so he drew his heavy mace,
And beat therewith on the Sultan's palace,
That he shattered the glass in the windows.
And the Sultan being in sore straits,
To his shame yielded his daughter to him.
The Arab sate him down and spake of the wedding:
"Fifteen white days will pass," quoth he,
"Or I may reach the level sea-coast,
And gather the gay wedding-guests."   80
Forthwith he mounted his slender mare,
And went forth to the level sea-coast
For to gather the gay-clad wedding-guests.
When the Sultan's daughter heard it,
She hissed like an angry snake:
"Dear God!" she cried, "Woe is me!
For whom have I been reared and tended?
For a black Arab, for to be his wife!"
But when dark night was come,
The Sultan's Sultana dreamed a dream,   90
And in the dream one spake to her, saying:
"There lieth within your empire
The wide plain of Kossovo,
And Prilep castle stands in the plain of Kossovo,
And in Prilep dwells Kraljević Marko,
And men praise him for a good knight of prowess.
Send therefore, a letter to Marko Kraljević,
Call him your son-in-the-true-God,
Promise him gold out of measure
If he but save your daughter from the Moor."   100
When day dawned on the morrow,
The Sultana ran to the Sultan's majesty,
And told what she had dreamed in her dream.
And when the Sultan understood her words,
With speed he wrote a firman,
And sent it to white Prilep,
Even to Kraljević Marko:

"Son-in-God, Kraljević Marko!
Come to me to white Stamboul;
Slay me this black Arab,   110
That he take not my daughter from me,
And I shall give thee three charges of gold."
The firman went to Kraljević Marko,
And when he received the firman,
And when he saw what was writ therein,
He said to the Sultan's courier[1]:
"God be with thee, thou royal messenger,
To the Sultan my father, greeting.
I dare not adventure me against the Moor,
For the Moor is a full perilous knight,   120
And if he should take the head from my shoulders,
Of what avail were three charges of gold?"
The courier went back to the illustrious Sultan,
And told what Marko had spoken.
When the Sultana heard it,
She indited another letter,
And sent it to Kraljević Marko:
"Son-in-God, Kraljević Marko,
Give not my daughter to the Moor,
And thou shalt have five charges of gold."   130
Marko Kraljević received the letter,
And when he saw what was writ therein,
He said to the imperial courier:
"Hie thee back, thou royal messenger!
Hie thee back, and tell my mother-in-God
I dare not adventure me against the Moor.
The Moor is a full perilous knight,
He will take the head from off my shoulders,
And I prefer mine own head
Before all the treasure of the illustrious Sultan."   140
The courier went back and told the Sultana
The words that Marko had spoken.
When the Sultan's daughter heard it,

---

[1] татарин = the Tatar, here signifying a mounted messenger.

Lightly she leapt to her feet,
And seized pen and paper.
She struck the pen into her face,
She drew blood from her cheek,
And wrote a letter to Marko:
"Brother-in-God, Kraljević Marko,
I call on thee as my brother-in-God,   150
And as my kum in God,
And in thine own Saint John,
Give me not over to the black Arab,
And thou shalt have seven charges of gold,
And a sevenfold present[1],
Not of things woven or spun,
Nor such as passeth through the weaver's loom,
But thy gifts shall be wrought of fine gold,
And I shall give thee a golden salver,
Whereon a twisted snake   160
Lifteth up his head on high,
Holding in his teeth a precious stone,
That shineth so as ye may sup by night
As it were by the light of day.
And I shall give thee a well-wrought sabre,
That hath a threefold hilt of gold,
Wherein be three precious stones.
The sabre is worth three of the Sultan's cities,
And I shall affix the Sultan's seal,
That the Vizier's self may not slay thee   170
Without he obtain permission of the illustrious Sultan."
She sent a courier with the letter to Marko.
When the letter came to Marko,
And he saw what the letter told him,
Forthwith Marko spake and said:
"Woe is me, my sister-in-God!
It were ill to go, and worse not to go,
For though I fear not Sultan nor Sultana,

[1] бошчалук = present given by bride to bridegroom and his near relations.

Of God and Saint John I am in sooth afeared.
Therefore will I follow this adventure to the utterance." 180
He sent back the courier without message,
For neither said he "I come," nor "I come not,"
But he went to the slender tower,
And did on gear meet for a journey.
About his shoulders he cast his cloak of wolf-skin,
On his head he set his cap of wolf-skin,
He girded on his well-forged sabre,
And took also his battle-spear.
He descended to Sharatz's stable,
And made fast the sevenfold saddle-girth. 190
Then he filled with wine a wine-skin,
And hanged it on the right side of Sharatz,
And on the left side he hanged his heavy mace,
That the saddle should not slip to this side nor to that.
Then he flung him on the back of Sharatz
And right so went forth to white Stamboul.
When he was come to white Stamboul,
He went neither to Sultan nor yet to Grand Vizier,
But to the new inn he went,
And there he would tarry the night; 200
But before the dark of night was come,
He led Sharatz to a lake,
For to water him with cold water.
But Sharatz would not drink of the water,
But looked ever round about him.
And behold a Turkish maiden,
Cloaked in a shawl of gold!
When the maiden drew nigh to the lake-side,
She bowed her down before the green lake.
"God aid thee, green lake," quoth she, 210
"God aid thee, my eternal home!
In thee I would be for ever!
Liever were I wedded with thee than with the Moor."
Then did Kraljević Marko make known his presence:
"Ha, Lady," quoth he, "thou Turkish maiden!

What is it that urgeth thee into the lake?
Wherefore wilt thou wed thee with the lake?
Into what sore straits art thou come?"
The Turkish maiden made answer:
"Let me pass, foul churl!   220
Wherefore dost thou ask since thou canst not help me?"
But she told him all from beginning to end,
How it was she sought refuge in the lake.
"And at the last," quoth she, "they spake to me of
  Marko,
That dwelleth in the castle of Prilep,
They said that Marko was a worthy knight,
That could slay the Arab an he would;
Therefore did I call him my brother-in-God,
I called him my kum-in-Saint-John,
And promised him many gifts of price. 230
In vain! Marko will not come,
He will not come, may his mother lose him!"
But Kraljević Marko spake and said:
"Curse me not, sister-in-God,
For thou seest Marko Kraljević in his proper person."
When the fair damsel heard it,
She threw her arms about Marko's neck.
"Brother-in-God, Kraljević Marko,
Give me not, I pray thee, to the black Arab!"
Answered her again Kraljević Marko: 240
"Sister-in-God, thou Turkish maiden,
Whilst my head is mine own,
I will not give thee to the black Arab.
Speak no word to any concerning me,
Save only to the Sultan and Sultana.
Let somewhat be prepared for my supper,
See that there be no stint of wine,
And let it be sent to me to the new inn.
And when the Moor cometh with his guests,
Let him receive fair welcome, 250
And let them give thee to the Moor,

That there be no brawling in the palace.
For I know how I shall save thee,
If God and knightly fortune prevail."
Right so went Marko to the new inn,
The damsel hied her to the Sultan's palace,
And told the Sultan and Sultana
That Kraljević Marko was come thither.
When the Sultan and the Sultana heard it,
They let make him a lordly supper,   260
Therewith also red wine out of measure,
And let carry it to the new inn.
Now while Marko sat drinking his wine,
They began to shut the houses in Stamboul city,
And now came the innkeeper for to close his doors,
And Kraljević Marko asked him:
"Wherefore dost thou close thus early?"
Straightway the innkeeper made answer:
"God save us, thou unknown knight!
A Moor hath wooed the Sultan's daughter,   270
And hath won her and shamed our Sultan,
And this night he cometh for the damsel.
Great is the terror of the Moor,
And for this cause we close thus early."
But Marko suffered not the door to be shut,
But stayed where he was that he might see the Moor,
And his gay-clad wedding-guests.
And now a sound arose in white Stamboul,
And behold the swarthy Moor,
Riding upon his slender Arab mare,   280
With five hundred wedding-guests with him,
Five hundred swarthy Arabs.
A Moor was dever, the chief guest[1] a Moor,
And a swarthy Moor was the bridegroom.
His mare bounded furiously beneath him,
That from her feet the stones flew up,
And beat upon shop and tavern.

[1] стари сват = the senior wedding-guest. See Appendix, p. 184.

When they were come before the new inn,
The Arab communed with himself:
"Dear God, what great marvel is this! 290
All Stamboul hath closed its doors
Because of the great terror of my name,
Alone the door of the new inn is not closed.
Whether doth no man lodge there?
Or is there any so dull and witless,
That he knoweth not yet of my renown?"
The Arab went to the Sultan's court,
And there through the dark night he tarried.
When day dawned on the morrow,
The Sultan led forth his daughter to the Arab; 300
The damsel's garments were made ready
And twelve pack-horses took the burden.
Across Stamboul went the Arab,
With the damsel and the wedding-guests with him.
When they were come before the new inn,
The door of the inn stood ever open.
The Moor urged forward his slender mare,
For to see who might be in the tavern;
And within the tavern sat Marko,
And ever the red wine he was drinking. 310
He drank not as men are wont to drink,
But he drank from a basin of twelve okas;
Himself drank half, and half he gave to Sharatz.
Fain would the Moor have picked a quarrel,
But Sharatz tethered to the doorpost,
Suffered him not to enter in,
But kicked his mare in the ribs.
The Moor returned to the wedding-guests,
And they went on together to the market-place.
Then arose Marko Kraljević, 320
He turned his wolf-skin cloak inside out,
Inside out his cap of wolf-skin;
He made fast the girths on Sharatz,
On one side he hanged a full wine-skin,

And he hanged his great mace on the other
Lest the saddle should slip this way or that.
He took also his battle-spear,
Then he sprang on the back of Sharatz,
And hied him to Stamboul market-place.
When he overtook the wedding-guests,   330
Forthwith he stirred up a conflict,
He drave through them that were behind to them that
    were before,
And when he had urged Sharatz nigh to the damsel,
He slew the kum and the dever.
Word was brought to the black Arab:
"Woe betide thee, black Arab!
A knight hath fallen upon thy wedding-guests;
His horse is not as other horses,
But piebald like as a cattle-beast;
Nor is the knight like as other knights,   340
He weareth a cloak of wolf-skin,
And on his head is a cap of wolf-skin;
In his teeth is something black
That is as large as a lamb of half a year.
When he came he stirred up conflict,
He drave through the guests from rear to front,
And he hath slain kum and dever!"
The Moor turned about his grey Arab mare,
And cried to Kraljević Marko:
"Woe betide thee, thou unknown knight!   350
Which devil hath persuaded thee,
That thou shouldst come among my wedding-guests,
And slay the kum and the dever?
Art thou a witless churl that knowest naught of me?
Or art thou a knight of worship that hath lost his reason?
Or is life become a weariness to thee?
By the faith of my body,
I shall gather up the reins of my mare,
Seven times shall I leap over thee,
Seven times over thee, and seven times back,   360

And then shall I smite off thy head!"
But Kraljević Marko answered:
"Lie me no lies, black Arab!
If God and knightly fortune will it,
Thou shalt not leap so far as now I stand,
How then shalt thou leap over me?"
Ah, hadst thou but seen the black Arab,
How he tugged at his mare's bridle,
And strake her with the sharp stirrup-irons!
For in good sooth was he minded to overleap him.   370
But the war-wise Sharatz suffered it not,
But rose up on his hind legs,
And on his fore-legs received the Arab mare;
With his teeth also he laid hold on her,
And rent off her right ear,
That the mare was all bathed in blood.
Ah, had one been there to see,
How hero ran in upon hero,
The swarthy Moor upon Kraljević Marko!
But neither might the Moor slay Marko,   380
Nor yet might Marko slay the Moor,
And ever the clash of sharp swords endured!
Thus, for four hours, they drave each against other.
And when the black Arab saw
That Marko was like to prevail against him,
He turned about his slender mare,
And fled across Stamboul market-place.
Marko pursued after him,
But swift was the wild Arab mare,
Swift was she, swift as the mountain Vila,   390
And well had she outstripped Sharatz,
But Marko bethought him of his mace;
He swung it round about and cast it,
And smote the Arab fair between the shoulders.
The Arab fell down, and when Marko was come,
He cut off the Arab's head,
And laid hold upon his slender mare.

Right with that he returned back through Stamboul
    market-place,
But of the wedding-guests there was none nowhere,
Alone remained the Sultan's fair daughter,   400
And round about her the twelve pack-loads,
That held fair garments of the damsel.
So Marko returned to the damsel,
And took her to the Sultan's palace,
And spake to the illustrious Sultan:
"Behold, Sultan, thy fair daughter!
And behold the head of the Arab!
Behold also the twelve pack-loads,
Wherein are the fair garments of the damsel."
Therewith he turned about his Sharatz,   410
And right so departed unto white Prilep.
When day dawned on the morrow,
The Sultan made ready seven charges of gold,
And the damsel prepared a sevenfold present,
Not of things woven or spun,
Nor of such as passeth through the weaver's loom,
But her gifts were wrought of fine gold.
She sent him a golden salver,
Whereon a twisted snake
Lift up his head on high,   420
And held in his teeth a precious stone,
That shone so as ye might sup by night
As it had been the light of day.
She sent him also a rich-wrought sabre,
That had a threefold hilt of gold,
Wherein were three precious stones.
Therewith, also, was the Sultan's seal,
That not the Grand Vizier durst do scathe to Marko,
Without the consentment of the illustrious Sultan.
All these she sent to Marko with the message: 430
"Behold, Marko, a little gold for thee,
And if ever thou shouldst lack for money,
Come again to the Sultan thy father."

MARKO KRALJEVIĆ AND MUSA THE OUTLAW[1]

Musa, the Albanian, was drinking wine
In Stamboul, in the white inn.
And when Musa had quaffed his fill,
Being drunken he spake a great word:
"Nine years already
Have I served the Sultan in Stamboul,
Nor have I gained by my service horse nor weapon,
Nor a new cloak nor yet an old one.
But I swear by all that is holy,
I shall go hence to the level coast,   10
I shall close the routes by sea,
And the roads by land.
I shall build a tower on the sea-coast,
And set it about with iron hooks,
And I shall hang thereon the hodjas and the hadjis[2]."
What the Turk said when he was drunken,
That sober he fulfilled:
To the level coast he betook him,
He closed the sea-routes round about,
And the roads by land,   20
By which the Sultan's treasure passed,
Each year three hundred tovars,
And Musa took it all for himself!
On the sea-coast he builded him a tower,
Round about the tower he set iron hooks,
And hanged thereon the Sultan's hodjas and hadjis.
Now when the Sultan was weary of complaints,
He sent against him the Vizier Ćuprilić,

---

[1] кесеџија = "latro turcicus equo vectus" (Vuk, *Dict.*). The word
comes from the Turkish кеса = a purse. Here the meaning of "highwayman" or "outlaw" is indicated.

[2] Hodja = "sacerdos turcicus" (Vuk).

Hadji = one who has made the pilgrimage to Mecca (or to Jeru-
salem in the case of a Christian) (Vuk).

With three thousand men with him.
But when they were come to the level sea-coast   30
Musa smote them all hip and thigh on the sea-coast.
He took captive the Vizier Ćuprilić,
He bound his hands behind his back,
He bound his feet beneath his horse,
And sent him to the Sultan in Stamboul!
The Sultan let summon proved knights,
And promised gold untold
To him that should slay Musa the Outlaw.
But whoso went forth on that quest,
He returned to Stamboul no more.   40
For that cause was the Sultan passing heavy,
But the hodja Ćuprilić spake to him, saying:
"Lord and master, Sultan of Stamboul,
Had we but with us Kraljević Marko,
He would slay thee this Musa."
The Sultan looked at him in anger,
And tears rolled down from his eyes:
"Enough," quoth he, "hodja Ćuprilić,
Wherefore dost thou speak of Kraljević Marko?
His very bones must or now be rotted.   50
For it is full three years of days,
Since I let cast him into prison,
Nor has the door once been opened."
Answered him the hodja Ćuprilić:
"An it please thee, Lord and master,
What wouldst thou give to the knight
That should show thee Marko alive?"
The Lord Sultan made answer to him:
"I should make him Vizier in Bosnia
For nine years without change,   60
Nor should I require of him a dinar nor yet a para."
The hodja leapt lightly to his feet,
He opened the door of the dungeon,
And led forth Kraljević Marko!
He led him forth before the illustrious Sultan:

His hair reached down to the black earth,
The half thereof served him for bed and half for coverlet;
With the nails of his fingers he could have ploughed,
The mould from the stone had gotten hold on him,
And he was become the colour of a dark stone.   70
The Sultan spake to Kraljević Marko:
"Art thou in good sooth alive, Marko?"
"Truly, Sultan," quoth he, "but in evil case."
Then the Sultan told Marko
The despite that Musa had done upon him,
And he asked Kraljević Marko:
"Canst thou take it upon thee, Marko,
To go down to the level coast-land
And slay Musa the Highwayman?
I will give thee gold as seemeth good unto thee."   80
Marko made answer to him:
"God's truth, my Lord Sultan!
The mould from the stone hath gotten hold on me
That I may not even see with mine eyes,
Much less strive with Musa body to body.
But set me in an inn somewhither,
Let serve me with wine and rakia,
With the flesh of fat rams,
And with loaves of white bread:
Let me remain there certain days,   90
And I shall tell thee when I am in case to fight."
The Sultan sent fetch three barbers,
One washed Marko, the second shaved him,
The third cut his finger-nails.
The Sultan set Marko in the new inn,
And let serve him with wine and rakia,
With the flesh of fat rams,
And with loaves of white bread.
And there Marko tarried three months of days,
Until his life was a little returned to him.   100
And the Sultan asked Kraljević Marko:
"Canst thou now take upon thee this adventure?

It wearies me of angry wretches,
That complain ever of that accursed Musa."
Marko said to the illustrious Sultan:
"Let bring dry cornel-wood
That has been nine years seasoning,
That I may see what I can bring out of it."
The Sultan let bring dry cornel-wood,
Marko gripped it in his right hand,   110
The wood crunching brake in two pieces and in three,
But no drop of water came forth of it.
"God's truth, Sultan," quoth he, "the time is not yet."
So there passed another month of days,
Until that Marko was somewhat refreshed,
And when him seemed he might now do battle,
He asked for dry cornel-wood,
And they brought Marko wood of the cornel.
And when he grasped it in his right hand,
It brast crunching in two pieces and in three   120
And there sprang forth two drops of water.
Right so, withal, Marko spake to the Sultan, saying:
"Sultan, the time is come."
Straightway he betook him to Novak the smith,
"Forge me a sabre, smith Novak," quoth he,
"Such as thou hast never forged before."
He gave him thirty ducats,
And gat him to the inn,
And there drank wine for three days and for four,
And then betook him once again to Novak: 130
"Hast thou forged me the sabre, Novak?" quoth he.
The smith brought out the weapon he had forged.
To him Kraljević Marko:
"Is it a good sword, smith Novak?"
And Novak answered and said:
"Lo, here is the sabre and here the anvil,
See for thyself what manner of sword it is."
Marko swung the sabre in his right hand,
And smote down upon the anvil,

And hewed the anvil in half.   140
Then he asked Novak the smith:
"In good sooth, Novak,
Hast thou ever forged a better blade?"
Novak the smith answered him again:
"In good sooth, Kraljević Marko,
I have forged one better,
A better sabre—for a better knight.
When Musa betook him to the coast-land,
I forged a sabre for him,
And when he smote down with it upon the anvil   150
Not even the block remained whole."
Thereat Kraljević Marko waxed wroth,
And thus to Novak the smith he spake:
"Stretch forth thy hand, Novak!
Stretch forth thy hand that I pay thee for the sabre."
The smith was deceived, the serpent of foolishnes bit him,
He was deceived, and he stretched forth his right hand.
Kraljević Marko swung the sabre
And hewed off his arm at the shoulder:
"Lo, here thy recompense, smith Novak!   160
Nevermore shalt thou make blades or better or worse.
And here for thee are an hundred ducats,
For to nourish thee the days of thy life."
He gave him an hundred ducats,
He mounted the war-tried Sharatz,
And hied him straightway to the level coast-land,
Where he went to and fro seeking word of Musa.
And on a morn as he journeyed early
Up the hard pass of Kačanik,
Lo, on a sudden, Musa the Outlaw!   170
Cross-legged he sat upon a black horse,
Tossing his mace to the clouds
And catching it in his white hand as it fell.
And when they drew nigh one to the other,
Marko spake to Musa and said:
"Bold Musa, get thee out of my way!

Get thee out of my way or do obeisance before me!"
But Musa the Albanian answered:
"Pass on thy way, Marko, and seek not to have ado
    with me,
Or light down if thou wilt, that we may drink wine
    together.   180
But I will not do obeisance before thee,
Albeit a queen bore thee,
In a čardak amongst soft cushions,
And wrapped thee in pure silk,
And bound thee about with thread of gold,
And nourished thee on honey and on sugar.
But as for me—a wild Arnaut[1] woman bore me,
Amongst the sheep on the cold ground.
In a rough black mantle she wrapped me,
And bound me about with thorns,   190
And nourished me on porridge.
Oft did she make me swear,
Never to give way to no man."
When Marko of Prilep heard it,
He cast his battle-spear
Between the ears of his Sharatz,
At the breast of the bold Musa.
Musa caught it on his mace,
And turned the spear aside from him.
Then took he his own battle-spear,   200
And cast it at Kraljević Marko.
Marko caught it on his mace
And brake the spear in three pieces.
Then they pulled out their sabres,
And ran furiously the one against other.
Marko Kraljević swung his sabre,
But the bold Musa thrust out his mace
And brake the sabre in three pieces;
Then quickly he pulled out his sword,
For to smite Marko Kraljević,   210

    [1] Arnaut = Albanian.

But Marko thrust out his mace
And brake off the blade at the hilt.
Then they seized their ribbed maces,
And therewith began to smite each the other,
That the ribbed maces brake,
And they cast them from them on the green grass.
They lighted down from their good horses,
They seized each other body to body,
And wrestled this way and that on the green grass.
For hero met hero in very sooth,   220
When Deli Musa met Kraljević Marko!
Nor might Musa overthrow Marko,
Nor by Marko might he be overthrown.
So they wrestled till noon of a summer's day;
White foam fell from Musa,
From Marko foam white and bloody.
And Musa the Outlaw spake and said:
"Overthrow me, Marko, or thee shall I overthrow."
Kraljević Marko put forth his strength,
But in no wise might he prevail.   230
Then Musa put forth his strength,
He overthrew Marko on the green grass,
And knelt upon the hero's breast.
Then Marko made grievous moan:
"Where art thou this day, sworn sister Vila?
Where art thou this day? Foul fall thee!
Falsely didst thou swear
Thou wouldst be with me to aid me,
If haply I should come into evil straits!"
From the clouds the Vila made known her presence: 240
"How now, brother Kraljević Marko!
Did I not lay charge upon thee,
To do no battle on the holy Sabbath?
It were shame also that two should prevail against one.
Bethink thee! Where are thy hidden fangs[1]?"
Musa looked up to the hills and to the clouds,

---

[1] *I.e.* "Where is thy concealed weapon?"

If haply he might know whence came the voice of the Vila.
Right so Marko drew forth a knife craftily,
And so he carved Musa the Outlaw
From the navel even to the white throat[1].   250
But the dead Musa lay heavy on Marko
That scarce might he win out from under him.
And when Marko had rolled Musa over,
He perceived in Musa three mighty hearts,
And three sets of ribs, one over other.
The first heart was quite spent,
The second throbbed strongly,
On the third slept an evil snake;
And when the snake awoke,
Dead Musa writhed on the greensward,   260
And the snake spake thus unto Marko:
"Give thanks to God, Kraljević Marko,
That I was not awaked from sleep
Whilst Musa was yet alive,
Else had three hundred woes come upon thee."
When Kraljević Marko saw this,
Tears ran down his face.
"God of Mercy," quoth he, "woe is me!
For I have slain a better than myself."
Then he strake off Musa's head,   270
And cast it into the corn-sack of Sharatz,
And bore it to white Stamboul.
When he cast down the head before the illustrious Sultan,
Sore adread the Sultan sprang to his feet,
And Kraljević Marko said to him:
"Be not adread, my Lord Sultan!
How hadst thou received him living,
When his dead head maketh thee so to leap?"
Three charges of gold the Sultan gave him;
Marko went forth to white Prilep,   280
Musa tarried on Kačanik.

---

[1] "Till he unseam'd him from the nave to the chaps," *Macbeth*,
Act I, Sc. 2.

Note. The story of three-hearted Musa was the legend referred to
by the signatories of an appeal by Jugo-Slavs against Italian pretensions.
"We offer friendship; they ask for obedience, proclaiming us bar-
barians....Conquerors behind the times, put not your hope in the
exhaustion of the Jugo-Slav race! If our nation spent its strength first
in the Balkan wars and then in this world war, its remaining power
of resistance has today increased by the hope of the union of all our
lands, and it will (like the hero in our legends who had three hearts)
wake to life with its third strength, to defend itself to the last breath rather
than bend its head under a new yoke." This document was signed
by Ivan Meštrovic and other distinguished artists and men of letters.

MARKO KRALJEVIĆ AND DJEMO THE MOUNTAINEER

K RALJEVIĆ MARKO celebrated his Slava,
He kept his Slava that fell on St George's day.
And many invited guests were there—
Two hundred priests, three hundred monks,
Twelve Serbian bishops,
Four patriarchs well stricken in years,
And others without number.
For all there was meat and drink and to spare,
Natheless an aged monk lift up his voice and said:
"Give thee thanks, Kraljević Marko!   10
There had nothing lacked in thy white manor,
An thou hadst fish from Ochrida[1]!"
Sore grieved was Kraljević Marko,
He called his servant Bogosav,
And gave him glass and wine-beaker:
"Pour thou the wine, Bogosav, my servant,
Give the glass in due order round the table,
See that thou pass not over any."
With that he gat him down from the white tower,
And made ready his war-horse Sharatz.   20
After him hasted his aged mother,
And spake (soft) words unto him:
"Ah, my son, Kraljević Marko,
Take not any weapon with thee,
Else—so used to blood art thou—
Thou wilt surely shed blood on thy festal day."
Lo, in a strait betwixt two was Marko!
Ill were it, him seemed, to go unarmed,
And yet more evil to give not heed to his mother.
So he took with him no weapon,   30
But mounted the war-tried Sharatz,
And steered him adown the grassland,

---

[1] The lake of Ochrida is celebrated for its fish.

And came with a straight course to white Ochrida.
Now when he was come to the river bridge,
Lo, a knight was there,
Seated cross-legged on a brown horse;
And ever he threw his battle-mace to the clouds,
And caught it again in his white hands.
"God aid thee," saith he to Marko,
And Marko gave him fair greeting again.   40
Then said the knight to Marko of Prilep:
"Tell me, I pray thee, stranger knight,
Art thou not come from Prilep,
From the manor of Kraljević Marko?
Is Marko in his white manor?
And hath he many invited guests there with him?"
Kraljević Marko made answer:
"In good sooth—thou stranger knight,
This morning was I at Prilep,
And Marko is indeed in his fair manor.   50
He celebrateth his patron saint,
And he hath many invited guests there with him."
The worshipful stranger knight answered him again:
"Though he have never so many, fair sir,
If God will and knightly fortune prevail,
His table shall swim in blood,
And by God, I will hang him,
Even on the gate of white Prilep.
For long since he slew my brother,
Musa, the outlaw."   60
So he urged his brown horse and went his ways,
And Marko's countenance was sore troubled.
This way and that he pondered, and his mind was divided;
For if he should make him known,
The Turk would surely slay him,
For that he had no weapon;
And if he suffered him to go his ways to Prilep,
The Turk would surely hew down many guests,
What time he sought Marko in his manor.

Many counsels he pondered, he resolved on one,   70
And so he cried with a loud voice:
"Whither goest thou, Djemo?
Lo, here am I, Kraljević Marko!"
Djemo, the Mountaineer, turned him about,
But Marko put his trust in Sharatz.
On his Sharatz he trusted he should have escaped,
And he fled away athwart the wide plain,
And Djemo followed hard after him;
Swift was Sharatz, and had right well escaped him,
But Djemo seized his battle-mace;   80
He wheeled it round him and cast it,
And smote Marko between the living shoulders.
Marko fell down on the green grass,
He fell and Djemo hasted to him
And bound his hands behind his back.
Then he drew forth the chain from the saddle-bag,
And bound him fast in bitter iron.
On his feet two fetters,
On his arms two armbands,
Round his neck the heavy chain of iron.   90
Then he mounted Marko's Sharatz,
And by the halter led the brown horse
Whereon he had bound Marko,
And came straightway to white Ochrida.
And by Ochrida he set up a gallows,
For there he purposed to hang Marko.
But the Christian lords besought him, saying:
"Brother-in-God, Djemo the Mountaineer,
Hang not Marko here,
Lest vine and wheat bear not any fruit.   100
Lo, here be three charges of gold!"
Djemo took the three charges of gold,
And led away Marko to Vučitern;
And by the town he set up a gallows,
For he purposed to hang Marko there.
But the Christian lords besought him, saying:

"Brother-in-God, Djemo the Mountaineer,
Hang not Marko here,
Lest vine and wheat bear not any fruit.
Lo, here be three charges of gold!"   110
Djemo took the three charges of gold,
And drave Marko further to white Zvečan.
And there Djemo set up a gallows,
For there he purposed to hang Marko.
But from Zvečan the lords came and besought him:
"Brother-in-God, Djemo the Mountaineer,
Hang not Marko here,
Lest vine and wheat bear not any fruit.
Lo, here be three charges of gold!"
Djemo took the three charges of gold,   120
And departed thence
Through a certain mountain called Janjina.
And Djemo was sore athirst,
And he spake (softly) to bold Marko:
"Knowest thou, Marko, if there be water here beside
     or any inn?
Sore thirst prevaileth over me."
To him answered Kraljević Marko:
"Knights of worship speak not on this wise, Djemo,
But rather they slay horse or falcon,
And stay their thirst with blood from the throat."   130
Djemo the Mountaineer made answer:
"Nor horse nor yet falcon will I slay,
But I am minded to slay thee, Kraljević,
For to stay my thirst with blood from thy throat."
Therewith he pulled out his well-wrought sabre,
Being in mind to slay Kraljević Marko.
But Kraljević Marko spake to him, saying:
"Soothly, Djemo, there is an inn hard by
And an accursèd ale-wife, Janja.
Now will Janja revenge herself of me.   140
Greatly of her wine have I drunken,
But have never given her a dinar."

Thereof was Djemo passing glad,
And right so they came before the inn.
And Janja the ale-wife came forth.
When she looked and saw Marko in fetters,
Marko winked at her with the eye,
And she laughed, Janja the ale-wife:
"Well done and featly, mighty man of men!
Thanks be to God for all that he hath wrought.   150
For that I have seen Marko bound in fetters
I will give thee to drink, Djemo,
Without white dinars nor yet paras.
Yea, for three white days if so it pleaseth thee."
She took Djemo's horse from him,
And brought him into the tavern,
And made him free of wine and rakia.
Djemo the Mountaineer drank deep,
And toasted the health of Marko Kraljević.
He toasted him but gave him naught to drink.   160
And when Djemo was grown merry with wine,
Janja the ale-wife brought him wine,
Red wine, seven years old;
Therein she put all manner of herbs,
And Djemo's head sank down to sleep unpillowed.
Lightly to her feet sprang Janja,
And loosed the irons from her pobratim.
And Marko fastened them upon Djemo.
And when he had made fast the heavy iron chain,
Marko sate him down to drink the red wine;   170
And he struck Djemo with boot and spur:
"Up, Djemo, let us drink together!"
Djemo the Mountaineer looked round about him,
He perceived Marko above him,
He felt the heavy iron chain about his neck.
Lightly sprang Djemo to his feet
But the chain of iron drew him down.
With arms and legs he strained,
His arms cracked in the shoulders,

And his legs cracked in the knee-joints,   180
But the hard iron held him.
Djemo sate him down on the black earth,
And Marko sat drinking the dark wine.
He drank to the health of Djemo the Mountaineer,
He drank to his health but gave him naught to drink.
And when Marko was flushed with wine,
He tied Sharatz to the brown horse,
And bound Djemo upon Sharatz,
Himself he mounted upon Djemo's brown
And went straightway to Vučitern.   190
Thence came forth to him Christian lords, saying:
"Brother-in-God, Kraljević Marko,
See that thou hang Djemo here.
Lo, here be three charges of gold!"
But Marko gave back to them the gold
That they had given to Djemo the Mountaineer,
And went on further to white Zvečan.
And the Christian lords came forth, saying:
"Brother-in-God, Kraljević Marko,
See that thou hang Djemo here.   200
Lo, here be three charges of gold!"
But Marko gave back to them the gold
That they had given to Djemo the Mountaineer,
And continued to white Ochrida.
And the Christian lords came forth, saying:
"Brother-in-God, Kraljević Marko,
See that thou hang Djemo here.
Lo, here be three charges of gold!"
And Marko would not take the gold,
But gave back to them the three charges   210
That they had given to Djemo the Mountaineer.
At Ochrida he builded a gallows,
And hanged Djemo the Mountaineer.
And he took fish from Ochrida lake,
And straightway gat him to white Prilep,
And there did honour to his patron saint.

MARKO KRALJEVIĆ ABOLISHES THE MARRIAGE-TAX

KRALJEVIĆ MARKO rode forth early,
Early he rode athwart the plain of Kossovo.
And when he was come to Servana river,
There met him a damsel of Kossovo.
And Marko gave her fair greeting:
"God aid thee, thou damsel of Kossovo!"
The damsel bowed her to the ground:
"Fair fall thee—stranger knight!"
Then Marko spake to her and said:
"Dear sister, damsel of Kossovo,   10
Right fair thou art—mayst thou wax younger!
Full seemly thou art of body and stature,
Rosy thy countenance, and high thy bearing.
But thy hair, sister, beseemeth thee not.
Wherefore art thou grown so grey?
By whom hast thou lost thy gladness?
Or by thine own fault or by thy mother's,
Or by the mean of thine aged father?"
The damsel of Kossovo wept tears,
And to Kraljević Marko she said: 20
"Dear brother, thou stranger knight,
Not by mine own fault am I unhappy,
Not by mine own fault nor because of my mother,
Nor yet because of mine aged father.
Natheless, miserable that I am, I have lost all gladness.
Lo, nine years of days are passed,
Since there came a Moor from beyond the sea,
And leased Kossovo from the Sultan,
And he inflicteth outrage upon Kossovo
That the folk give him meat and drink out of measure.   30
In this too he doeth violence—
For every woman that would wed must pay him thirty
    ducats,

And every man four and thirty.
Whosoever hath the money and will pay the full tale thereof,
Such an one may take to him a wife,
Such a damsel may dare to be wedded.
But as for me, my brothers are poor men,
No gold had they to give to the Moor,
Wherefore was I left forlorn,
Nor might not wed me.   40
And for that have I lost all gladness,
Yet not therefor would I make such dole and sorrow,
That he suffereth us not to be married,
Nor to wed with the knights our lovers,
But lo, another grief and a greater!
A greater shame the Moor hath put upon us,
For each night he will have a young wife, and a maiden also,
And the Moor embraceth the maiden,
And his servants take the young wife.
And all Kossovo must send him in appointed turn,   50
Their young wives and their maidens also,
And behold, wretched that I am, mine own turn is come,
And this night I must thither to the Moor,
That he may lie with me this night.
And I think and ponder many thoughts,
Dear God, what shall I do and how?
Unhappy that I am, shall I leap into the river,
Or shall I hang myself?
For, brother, I had liever lose my head,
Than embrace my country's foe!"   60
But Kraljević Marko spake and said:
"Dear sister, damsel of Kossovo!
Speak not foolishly, leap not into the river,
Deal not death unto thyself.
I pray thee, sister, lay not this sin upon thy soul!
But say me where is the Moor's manor,
Where is the manor of the black Moor?
I have words to speak with him."
Quoth the damsel:

"Dear brother, thou stranger knight,   70
Wherefore dost thou ask of the Moor's manor?
Wherefore askest thou? May it be utterly laid waste!
Haply thou hast found a maiden,
And goest now thither bearing the tax-money.
Haply thou art the only son of thy mother,
And wit thou well, brother, thou goest yonder to thy death,
And how then will thy mother nourish her?"
Marko put his hand in his pocket,
He took out thirty gold ducats
And gave them to the damsel of Kossovo: 80
"Behold, sister, thirty ducats for thee.
And now get thee to thy white manor,
There continue until good fortune greet thee[1].
Tell me only where the Moor's manor lieth,
I would fain pay thy marriage-tax.
And wherefore should the Moor slay me,
Since that I have gold and to spare?
I could pay for all Kossovo plain!
Is it then hard for me to pay thy tax?"
Quoth the damsel: 90
"No manor hath the Moor but niggard tents.
Look down over Kossovo,
Where yonder silken banner waves.
There is the tent of the black Moor.
Round about it is a green pleasance,
And all the pleasance is garnished with heads!
Lo, not a week of days agone
The accursed Moor did slay
Seventy and seven heroes,
Unhappy bridegrooms of Kossovo!   100
Forty servants hath the Moor,
That stand round him to watch over him."
And when Marko heard these words,
He urged Sharatz and went down to Kossovo.
He spurred good Sharatz to fury,

      [1] *I.e.* "until a suitor cometh for thee."

That living fire flashed from his hoofs,
And a blue flame went from his nostrils.
In wrath rode Marko athwart Kossovo,
Tears ran down the hero's face,
And wrathful through his tears he spake: 110
"Ah me! Thou Kossovo plain,
What ills are come upon thee now,
Since the days of our illustrious prince[1],
That Moors should sit in judgment over thee!
But this shame I may not suffer,
Nor endure the heaviness thereof,
That the Moors do us this great despite,
And lie with our brides and young maidens!
This day, my brethren, I shall revenge you,
I shall revenge you, or I will perish!"   120
Right so Marko went towards the tents,
And the Moorish guard perceived him,
And said to the black Moor:
"Lord and master, Moor from beyond the sea!
A marvellous knight rideth down to Kossovo,
On a passing great piebald horse,
And he hath spurred him to fury,
That living fire flasheth from his hoofs,
And a blue flame goeth from his nostrils.
This knight is surely minded to make onfall on us."   130
But the black Moor made answer:
"My children—my forty henchmen,
There is no knight that dareth to make onfall on us,
It is like that he hath found a damsel,
And hasteth to us bearing the marriage-tax:
He is grieved that he must needs yield up the gold,
And for that cause is he wroth out of measure.
Go ye out now before our courtyard,
And receive the knight well and seemly,
And do humble obeisance before him.   140
Take from him his good steed,

[1] Tsar Lazar.

His steed and his weapons likewise,
And suffer him then to enter into my tent.
I seek not his gold but I will have his head
That I may possess a horse that is worthy of me."
Then the Moor's henchmen went out
For to take Marko's trusty steed;
But when they saw Marko near at hand,
They durst not go to him.
So they fled into the Moor's tent 150
And hid them behind the Moor their master.
They covered their swords with their mantles,
Lest Marko might be ware of their weapons.
Alone entered Marko into the courtyard,
Before the tent he lighted down from Sharatz,
And to his trusty Sharatz thus he spake:
"Go thou, Sharo, to and fro within this courtyard,
For I will into the tent of the Moor,
But be thou ever by the door of the tent,
Lest I be put in jeopardy." 160
Therewithal Marko went into the tent,
And the Moor sat there drinking cool wine,
And a young bride and a maiden served him.
And Marko gave him fair greeting:
"God aid thee, noble lord!"
The Moor returned him yet fairer salutation:
"Long life to thee, fair stranger, and worshipful knight!
Come, Sir Knight, let us drink wine together,
Then shalt thou tell me wherefore thou art come."
But Kraljević Marko said: 170
"I have not time to drink with thee,
But I am come to thee of good intent,
Of better intent might no man be;
I have wooed a fair damsel,
The wedding-guests are on the road here beside,
And I am come bearing the tax-money,
That I may pay the money and lead home the damsel,
No man daring to stand in the way.

Tell me, how much is the marriage-tax?"
Then the Moor answered Marko fairly: 180
"Thou knowest it this long time already,
Whosoever taketh a husband payeth thirty ducats,
And whoso taketh a wife payeth four and thirty.
But meseemeth thou art a noble knight of prowess,
And it will do thee no hurt to give an hundred."
Marko felt with his hand in his pockets,
And threw down before the Moor three ducats:
"Trust me," quoth he, "no more gold have I,
But and if thou mayst endure
Till I am returned home with the fair damsel,   190
Then will rich presents be given to me,
And unto thee shall I give them all.
To thee the presents, to me the maiden."
The Moor gnashed like an angry snake:
"From me, thou whore, thou gettest no credit,
Thou givest not the gold and wouldst mock me withal."
Right on that he seized his heavy mace
And smote Kraljević Marko,
Three times he smote him, yea, and four times!
Kraljević Marko laughed: 200
"O worshipful black Moor," quoth he,
"Art jesting or smitest thou in good earnest?"
The Moor gnashed like an angry snake:
"I jest not," he said, "but smite in earnest."
Quoth Marko:
"I weened that thou didst but jest, thou felon knight,
But since thou dost smite in good earnest,
Wit ye well that I also have a mace
Wherewith to smite thee three, yea, and four times.
For as oft as ye have smitten me,   210
So often shall I smite thee again.
Then shall we go forth of the tent,
For to fight together to the utterance."
Marko drew his battle-mace,
And smote the black Moor,

And how lightly so ever he smote him,
He strake off his head from his shoulders!
Kraljević Marko laughed:
"Dear God," quoth he, "thanks be to thee in all things!
As swiftly went this knight's head from him   220
As if head he had never borne."
Then he pulled out his sabre from his girdle,
And one after other he smote the Moorish servants.
The forty servants he cut in pieces,
But four only that he would save alive.
And he saved them that they should bear true witness,
That they should say the truth to all men,
How it was with Marko and the Moor.
Then he took down all the heads from the pleasance,
And gave them fair burial,   230
That the eagles and the ravens should not rend them.
Then the bare pleasance again he garnished,
He garnished it with the heads of the Moors:
And he took the Moor's treasure,
And called to him the four servants
Whom he had saved alive,
And he sent them athwart Kossovo,
North, and south, and east and west he sent them.
And the Moor's servants made proclamation through-
     out Kossovo:
"If there be any maid of age to wed,   240
Let her seek unto herself a lord.
Let her marry in the days of her youth.
And if any knight would take to him a wife,
Let him seek a sweetheart and let him marry.
Henceforth there is no marriage-tax,
For Marko hath paid for all."
And all the people, both great and small, cried:
"God keep Kraljević Marko,
Who hath delivered the land from evil,
Who hath utterly destroyed the oppressor: 250
God save him, both soul and body!"

MARKO'S HUNTING WITH THE TURKS

MURAD the Vizier went a-hunting,
In the green mountain he went a-hunting,
With a brave fellowship of twelve,
And as thirteenth, Kraljević Marko.
Three white days they hunted,
Nor any quarry might they find.
And it fortuned that chance brought them
To a green lake in the forest[1],
Wherein swam ducks of golden wing.
And the Vizier loosed his falcon,   10
For to take a duck of golden wing.
But the duck tarried not in his sight,
But soared upward to the clouds,
And the falcon perched him in a green fir-tree.
Then spake Kraljević Marko:
"Is it permitted, Murad Vizier,
That I loose now my falcon,
For to take yonder duck of golden wing?"
Quoth Murad the Vizier:
"Yea, verily it is permitted, Marko, and wherefore not?"   20
Marko loosed his falcon,
He flew up into the clouds,
And seized the duck of golden wing,
And dropped with her under the green fir-tree.
And when the Vizier's falcon saw this,
He was grieved out of measure,
For he was wont to use an evil custom,
And take the quarry that another had won.
Right so he sped to Marko's falcon,
For to take from him the duck of golden wing;   30

[1] Гора is used indifferently to mean either a mountain or a forest.
The reason is that Serbia is both mountainous and well-wooded, so the
two ideas are closely associated.

But full stiff-necked[1] was Marko's falcon,
Even as his lord and master,
He yielded not up the duck of golden wing,
But strake the Vizier's falcon,
And strewed abroad his grey feathers.
And when Murad perceived it,
He was wonderly wroth,
And forthwithal he took Marko's falcon,
And dashed him against the green fir-tree,
That he brake his right wing.   40
And with that Murad returned back through the green-
    wood,
With his brave fellowship of twelve with him.
Marko's falcon hissed
Like angry snakes among the rocks.
Marko took his falcon,
And began to bind up his wing,
And with wrathful voice he said:
"Alas for thee and for me, falcon,
To go on hunting with the Turks without fellowship
    of Serbs,
For so they give us but a sorry share."   50
When he had bound up the falcon's wing,
Marko sprang on the back of Sharatz,
And pursued after through the black forest.
Sharatz went like the mountain Vila,
Swift and far he went,
And within a while they came to the edge of the dark
    forest,
And on the plain below they saw the Vizier,
With his fellowship of twelve with him.
The Vizier Murad looked about him,
And when he was ware of Kraljević Marko,   60
He said to his fellowship:
"My children, my brave fellowship of twelve,

---

[1] "Stiff-necked"; јогуница is rendered as "der Eigensinnige" in
Vuk's *Dict.*, also as "pertinax."

Ye see yonder wreath of mist,
Yonder mist wreath by the dark forest?
In yonder mist is Kraljević Marko,
See to what madness he hath urged Sharatz!
God wot—this bodeth but little good."
Right so Marko came thither,
He pulled out his sword from his thigh,
And ran upon Murad the Vizier.   70
The brave fellowship fled athwart the plain,
As sparrows flee to the thicket before the sparrow-hawk.
But Marko overtook Murad,
And hewed off his head,
And of the twelve companions,
He made four and twenty.
Then Marko fell to pondering,
Whether were better to seek the Sultan at Jedren[1],
Or to hie him to Prilep to his own white manor.
And when he had well considered, he said: 80
"It were better to go to Jedren to the Sultan,
And tell him what I have done,
Than to suffer the Turks first to make accusation
    against me."
When Marko was come to Jedren,
And was entered into the Divan into the Sultan's presence,
His eyes grew blurred in his head
Like the eyes of a famished wolf in the forest.
And when he looked, it was as if lightning flashed.
The Sovereign Sultan asked him, saying:
"My son, Kraljević Marko,   90
Wherefore art thou come in such sore anger?
Art thou in lack of money?"
Then Marko began to speak to the Sultan,
And he told him all as it had come to pass.
When the Sultan had heard Marko,
He burst out laughing,
And said to him:

      [1] Adrianople.

"Go to, thou hast done well, my son Marko!
Hadst thou not done on this wise,
I had called thee my son no more.   100
Any Turk may become Vizier,
But there is no knight of prowess like unto Marko!"
Then he felt in his silken pockets,
And drew forth a thousand ducats,
And gave them to Kraljević Marko:
"This for thyself," quoth he, "Son Marko,
Go and drink wine to thy heart's content."
Marko took the thousand ducats,
And went forth of the imperial Divan.
Now the Sultan gave not Marko the ducats,   110
That he should drink red wine,
But that he should get him out of his sight,
For of Marko's anger he was sore adread.

MARKO DRINKS WINE IN RAMADAN

Sultan Suleiman let cry an order
That none should drink wine in Ramadan,
That none should wear green apparel,
That none should bear a sword,
That none should dance with women in the kolo[1].
But Marko danced with women in the kolo,
Marko girded on his well-forged sabre,
Marko garbed himself in green apparel,
Marko drank red wine in Ramadan.
And he forced the hodjas and the hadjis,   10
That they also drank the wine-cup with him.
And there went Turks to seek judgment of the Sultan:
"Sultan Suleiman," said they, "our father and our
        mother!
Hast thou not let cry an order
That none should drink wine in Ramadan,
That none should wear green apparel,
That none should bear a sword,
That none should dance with women in the kolo!
Yet Marko danceth in the women's kolo,
Marko girdeth on his well-forged sabre,   20
Marko garbeth him in green apparel,
Marko drinketh wine in Ramadan!
Did he drink alone it were no great matter,
But he compelleth the hodjas and the hadjis,
That they also drink wine with him."
And when the Sultan understood these words,
He sent two on a message to Marko:
"Go forth," quoth he, "ye two messengers,
Say to Kraljević Marko,
That the Sultan biddeth him to the Divan."   30
The two messengers went forth,

    [1] Kolo, lit. a wheel. Serb national dance.

And when they were come to Kraljević Marko,
Behold, Marko sat in his tent drinking,
And before him was a tankard of twelve okas[1].
Unto him the two messengers spake, saying:
"Hearken unto us, Kraljević Marko!
The Sultan biddeth thee to the Divan,
In the Divan must thou appear before him."
Therewithal Marko waxed passing wroth,
He seized the tankard with the wine therein,   40
And smote the Sultan's messengers,
That their heads brast and the tankard also,
And blood and wine were mingled together!
To the Sultan's Divan went Marko,
And sate him down by the right knee of the Sultan.
His cap of sable he pulled down over his eyes,
His mace he kept fondling ever,
And his sabre he laid across his knees.
And Sultan Suleiman spake to him: ·
"My son, Kraljević Marko!   50
I did let cry an order,
That none should drink wine in Ramadan,
That none should wear green apparel,
That none should bear a sword,
That none should dance with women in the kolo.
Yet there are that say ill of thee, Marko,
And bear false witness against thee,
That thou dancest with women in the kolo,
That thou bearest thy sabre,
That thou goest garbed in green apparel,   60
That thou drinkest wine in Ramadan,
And further thou constrainest hodjas and hadjis,
That they should drink wine with thee!
And wherefore now hast thou pulled thy kalpak over
        thine eyes?
Wherefore dost thou toy with thy mace?
Wherefore is thy sabre laid across thy knees?"

[1] 12 okas = 6 gallons.

Quoth Kraljević Marko:
"Father, Sultan Suleiman,
If I drink wine in Ramadan,
If indeed I drink, my faith alloweth it;   70
If I put constraint on the hodjas and the hadjis
It is that for very shame
I may not drink while they do naught but look.
Let them not come to me to the inn.
And if I wear green apparel,
I am young and it liketh me well.
If I bear my rich-wrought sabre,
With mine own gold I bought it,
And if I dance with women in the kolo,
It is that I have no wife of mine own,   80
And thou too, Sultan, wert once unwed.
If I have pulled my kalpak over mine eyes,
The forehead sweats when the Sultan frets,
And I toy with my mace,
And lay my sabre in my lap,
Because I fear that strife may come of this;
And if strife should come,
Woe to him that is nearest Marko!"
The Sultan looked about him on every side
If haply there should be any nearer to Marko;   90
But near Marko there was none other,
But the Sultan Suleiman was nearest of all.
The Sultan gave back a little, Marko followed after,
Until he drave him to the wall.
Then the Sultan put his hand in his pocket
And drew forth an hundred ducats,
And gave them to Kraljević Marko.
"Go, Marko," quoth he, "drink wine to thy heart's
    content."

THE TURKS COME TO MARKO'S SLAVA

K RALJEVIĆ MARKO prayed God ever,
From year to year again,
That with pomp and splendour he might hold his Slava,
On Saint George's summer day,
And that the Turks should not come to his Slava.
Now when Saint George's day was come,
All the lords he bade to the Slava,
And in his manor he set out three tables;
At the first table were twelve bishops,
At the second were the Christian lords,   10
At the third were the poor and needy.
Marko served wine to the priests,
And to the worshipful Christian lords,
And his mother served the poor and needy,
And Jelitsa bore the sweetmeats.
Vaistina he set on guard,
For to keep watch against the Turks,
That the Turks should not come to the Slava.
And there drew nigh three Turkish Agas,
With thirty janissaries with them,   20
And the three Agas of the Sultan cried with a loud voice,
And the thirty janissaries with them:
"Giaour, open the gate!
That we may see, witless Giaour,
How Marko celebrateth his Slava."
The servant made goodly answer in the Turkish tongue:
"Open for yourselves, Turkish janissaries!
I dare not open the door,
For I fear my lord and master."
The Turks recked little enough of that,   30
But they plucked out thirty maces,
And brake down the door in the gate,
And on the servant's shoulders were counted out

Strokes six and thirty of golden maces.
To the good servant they made soft the back,
And when it wearied the hero of fighting,
And his shoulders were grown stiff,
He went weeping into the castle to Marko.
Marko Kraljević said to him:
"Vaistina, my dear child,   40
Wherefore, son, dost thou shed these tears?
Art thou anhungered or art athirst, my son?
If thou art anhungered, here be victuals,
If athirst, lo, here is cool wine.
Shed not these great tears,
For so thou doest despite to my patron saint."
And the servant Vaistina said:
"Lord and master, Kraljević Marko,
Neither am I anhungered nor yet athirst.
Evil have I gotten with the bread that I have eaten,   50
And worse evil with the wine that I have drunken
In thy lordly manor, Marko!
Thou sentest me to keep watch and ward,
But who would keep watch and ward for thee?
There came three Turkish Agas
With thirty janissaries with them,
And the three Agas called with a loud voice:
'Giaour, open the gate!
That we may see, witless Giaour,
How Marko celebrateth his Slava.'   60
And in Turkish made I fair answer:
'Open for yourselves, Turkish janissaries!
I dare not open the door,
For I fear my lord and master.'
The Turks recked little enough of that,
They plucked out thirty maces,
They brake down the door of the gate,
And they paid out on to my shoulders,
Strokes six and thirty of golden maces."
When Marko heard these words,   70

He took his sabre and his mace,
And before his guests he swore:
"Hearken, my lords and guests,
I am not the son of my mother,
The illustrious queen,
If I garnish not Prilep,
Not with basil nor yet with red roses,
But with a row of Turkish heads."
Then his mother began to beseech him,
The illustrious queen spake and said: 80
"Stay thee, Marko, my dear child!"
And right so the mother made bare her breast, saying:
"Lest thy mother's milk slay thee,
Do no deed of blood this day.
This day is thy glorious Slava,
If any enter into thy manor this day,
Give drink to the thirsty, give food to the hungry,
For the souls of thy parents,
And for the weal of thine own soul and Jelina's[1]."
Marko gave heed to his mother,   90
He put by his sabre but put not his mace aside,
So the Turks entered into the manor to their scathe.
And he set them in order round the table.
"Vaistina," quoth Marko, "give them to drink,
Jela, my soul, give them to eat."
The servant brought wine and rakia,
And Jelitsa brought goodly viands,
So they were of good cheer and drank wine.
And when the Turks had drunk a little,
They said among themselves in Turkish: 100
"Brethren, let us hence!
Before the viands stick in our throats."
The Turks thought that Marko knew not Turkish,
But Marko had been at the Sultan's court
Beyond the sea in Syria of the Turks,

[1] In "Djemo the Mountaineer" Jevrosima gives expression to the
same sentiments, and in each case Marko gives way to her.

And had dwelt there seven years,
And had learnt fine Turkish,
As if a Turkish mother had borne him.
And Marko said to the Turks:
"Sit ye down, Turks, drink wine!   110
Pay me the leech's fee for my servant;
But if ye will not do so,
Wait until I reach you
But one buffet apiece with my mace.
There is but little substance therein,
Forty okas of cold iron,
Twenty fair okas of clear silver,
And six okas of beaten gold;
In all six and sixty okas.
And I let you wit that well have ye earned it,   120
For ye did break down my door,
And did count out on my servant's shoulders
Six and thirty blows of golden maces."
Therewith an ague took all the Turks,
For fear of Marko's terrible mace.
Each one drew forth twenty ducats,
And the Agas drew forth thirty ducats.
They put the ducats on the hem of Marko's garment,
For so they hoped Marko would leave them in peace,
But he would in no wise leave them.   130
Marko, the Giaour, drank wine,
Fain would he have picked a quarrel with the Turks:
"Ho, Turks, sit ye down and drink,
And do ye give me somewhat in return.
My Jela is not a slave,
She has soiled the silken robe she wears
While serving you with goodly viands."
And now the Turks were in straits,
For already some lacked money,
And one borrowed from another.   140
Each one yielded up ten ducats,
And the Agas gave twenty ducats apiece.

They put the money on the hem of Marko's garment,
Then he gathered it with his hand into his pockets,
And went to his mother's apartments singing,
To the apartments of his mother, Jevrosima:
"Jevrosima, mine aged mother,
I took not gold from the Turks,
I took not gold because I had no gold,
But I took gold from the Turks   150
That it should be said and sung,
How Marko dealt with the Turks!"
The Turks went weeping from the manor;
The Turks spake in Turkish together, saying:
"God slay the Turk
That should henceforth go to any Giaour
What time the Giaour keepeth Slava.
What we have given for a single dinner,
Would well have nourished us for a year of days!"

MARKO'S PLOUGHING

KRALJEVIĆ MARKO sat at wine,
    With the aged Jevrosima his mother.
And when they had enough drunken,
Marko's mother spake to him, saying:
"O my son, Kraljević Marko,
Cease, my son, from thy adventures,
For evil may bring no good thing with it,
And it wearies thine aged mother,
That she must ever be washing bloody garments.
So take thou plough and oxen,   10
Plough hill and valley,
Then sow, my son, fair wheat,
And thus shalt thou feed both thee and me."
Marko hearkened unto his mother,
He took plough and oxen,
But he ploughed not hill nor valley,
But he ploughed the Sultan's highway.
And there passed that way Turkish janissaries,
Having three charges of gold with them,
And they said to Kraljević Marko: 20
"Go to, Marko, plough not the highway!"
"Go to, Turks," quoth he, "spoil not my ploughing!"
"Go to, Marko, plough not the highway!"
"Go to, Turks, spoil not my ploughing!"
And when it wearied Marko of words,
He swung plough and oxen on high,
And slew therewith the Turkish janissaries.
Then he took the three charges of gold,
And brought them to his mother,
"Behold," quoth he, "what I have ploughed for thee
    this day."   30

THE MARRIAGE OF DJURO OF SMEDEREVO

WHEN Djuro of Smederevo married him,
He wooed a king's daughter afar off,
In the fair city of Dubrovnik,
Whereof Michael was king,
And his daughter's name was Jerina[1].
Djuro wooed her, the King gave her to him.
In his wooing of the fair damsel,
Djuro spent three charges of gold;
In gifts also for the mother and sister of his bride,
He spent a thousand golden ducats.   10
When he began to talk of the wedding-day,
Then the King answered Djuro, saying:
"Hearken to me, Djuro of Smederevo,
When thou art come to thy castle of Smederevo,
And goest about to gather thy wedding-guests,
See that thou ask not Serbs as wedding-guests,
For overmuch do the Serbs love drinking,
And of brawling also are they overfond.
They would get drunken, they would raise strife and
    tumult,
And if thou mightst not stay the strife,   20
Small hope were thine to lead forth my daughter!
Therefore do thou summon Greeks and Bulgars,
Gather of them as many as ye will,
And come for the damsel when it pleaseth thee."
When Djuro of Smederevo heard it,
He made him ready to go forth of the white palace,
And took his journey toward Smederevo:
But on his way thither a letter overtook him,
From Jerina the fair damsel:
"Hearken to me, Djuro of Smederevo,   30
When thou art come to white Smederevo,
And goest about to gather thy wedding-guests,

---

[1] Jerina founded the fortress of Avala. Cf. Mijatovich.

Heed not the words of my father,
Summon neither Greeks nor yet Bulgars,
Or never wilt thou go forth alive
Out of our city of Dubrovnik,
Nor never mayst thou lead home thy bride!
So do thou ask Serbs to be thy wedding-guests,
As kum take Novak Debelić,
As prikumak, Gruja Novaković,   40
As stari svat, Janko of Sibinj,
As dever, Marko Kraljević,
As čauš, the wingéd Relja,
As vojvoda, Miloš Obilić,
As barjaktar, Milan Toplica,
As privenac, Ivan Kosančić.
As for the others, ask whom ye will;
Gather together, Djuro, a thousand guests,
And come as soon as it liketh thee."
When Djuro had scanned the letter,   50
He had little pleasure of it,
And came in a study to Smederevo.
While he was yet afar off,
His mother spied him,
And came out for to meet him;
They embraced and kissed each the other,
And Djuro kissed his mother's hand.
Then each took other by the hand,
And so they entered into the white manor,
And sate them down at the well-spread sofra.   60
And Djuro's mother asked him:
"Son of mine, Djuro, Djuro of Smederevo!
Art thou come to me in peace?
Hast thou won for me a daughter-in-law?
For me a daughter, for thee a faithful wife?"
Answered to her Djuro Smederevac:
"God be praised, mine aged mother!
I have journeyed in peace hither;
A daughter have I won for thee,

For thee a daughter, for myself a faithful wife,   70
In the fair city of Dubrovnik,
Whereof Michael is king.
I have won the King's daughter, the damsel Jerina.
And in wooing the damsel Jerina,
I have spent three charges of gold.
In gifts also for her mother and sister,
I have spent a thousand ducats;
And when I spake of the wedding-day,
Then said the King to me—
That when I went about to gather the wedding-guests, 80
I should ask no Serbs as wedding-guests.
'Overmuch,' quoth he, 'do the Serbs love drinking,
And of brawling also are they overfond.
They will get drunken, they will raise strife and tumult,
Thou wilt not avail to stay the strife,
How thinkest thou then to lead forth my daughter?
Therefore do thou summon Greeks and Bulgars,
Gather of them as many as ye will,
And come for the damsel when it pleaseth thee.'—
I departed thence, mother,   90
And on the road a letter reached me
From Jerina, my bride, saying—
'Hearken to me, Djuro of Smederevo,
When thou art come to white Smederevo,
And goest about to gather thy wedding-guests,
Heed not the words of my father,
Summon neither Greeks nor yet Bulgars,
Or never wilt thou go forth alive
Out of our city of Dubrovnik,
Nor never mayst thou lead home thy bride!   100
But do thou ask Serbs to be thy wedding-guests:
As kum take Novak Debelić,
As prikumak, Gruja Novaković,
As stari svat, Janko of Sibinj,
As dever, Marko Kraljević,
As čauš, the wingéd Relja,

As vojvoda, Miloš Obilić,
As barjaktar, Milan Toplica,
As privenac, Ivan Kosančić,
As for the others, ask whom ye will,   110
Gather together, Djuro, a thousand guests,
And come hither as soon as it liketh thee.'—
Counsel me now, mother,
Whether should I obey the King, my father-in-law,
Or the maid, Jerina, his lovely daughter?"
His mother answered him, saying:
"Dear son, Djuro of Smederevo,
The Latins were ever deceivers,
And fain, my son, would they deceive thee.
Hearken not to the King thy father-in-law,   120
But obey the word of thy bride Jerina.
Do thou ask Serbs to be thy wedding-guests,
And if haply thou art in straits,
They will be with thee in thy need."
When Djuro of Smederevo heard it,
He sate him down and on his knee he wrote letters,
And sent them forth everywhither.
Then he rested him certain days,
And behold there came Starina Novak,
And his son Grujica with him;   130
Thereafter but a little time,
Behold Janko of Sibinj,
With an hundred wedding-guests with him;
And Janko entered into the white manor;
Then across the fields appeared Marko,
And after Marko, Relja of Pazar,
And after Relja, Miloš the vojvoda,
After Miloš, Milan Toplica,
And after Milan, Ivan Kosančić.
So the Serb knights assembled together,   140
With a thousand well-beseen guests with them.
Fair welcome indeed they had of Djuro,
And he spake them words of counsel, saying:

"Ye thousand guests, my brothers!
I go not mine own self to Dubrovnik,
But I send my pobratim, Marko;
See that ye do well obey Marko,
And my kum also, Starina Novak."
So the wedding-guests departed thence,
And journeyed in peace to Dubrovnik.   150
And when they were come to Dubrovnik city,
Kraljević Marko spake and said:
"Ye thousand guests, my brothers!
Now shall we go in at the gates,
And we must pass, dear brothers,
Gates seven and seventy[1],
Before we may come at the white castle.
And before the castle they have laid tables,
They have set wine and rakia thereon,
And of fine meats every sort;   160
About the tables be serving-men and maids,
For to take your horses and your weapons,
Ye will give them your horses, your weapons ye will not
      give,
But ye will sit down armed at the tables,
And drink the dark wine above your weapons;
When the King of Dubrovnik cometh,
Be ye silent, for I will speak with him."
Therewithal they arrived before the castle,
The menservants took their horses,
And the maidservants would take their shining weapons: 170
They gave up their horses, their weapons they did not give,
But they sat down armed at the tables,
And drank the dark wine across their weapons.
And behold the King of Dubrovnik cometh,
Fair words he spake to them, saying:
"Fair Sir, most worshipful Novak,
Never or now have I seen wedding-guests

[1] A favourite expression to denote vaguely any large number. See
"The Sister of Leka Kapetan."

That sat weaponed at their wine."
Novak held his peace, no word said he,
But Kraljević Marko spake and said: 180
"Fair sweet Sir, thou King of Dubrovnik!
This is the custom of the Serbs,
For they use to drink their wine across their weapons,
And beside their weapons they seek sleep at night."
The king turned him about and went back into the castle.
There they spent the dark night,
And when day dawned on the morrow,
A Latin stripling cried aloud from the wall:
"Hear ye, Novak Debelić!
Lo, yonder in the white tower be two Latins   190
That would fain joust with thee,
And thou must needs go forth to them in the field,
And then shall ye lead away the damsel Jerina."
When Starina Novak heard it,
He looked at his son Grujica,
And Grujica looked not to the right nor to the left,
But leapt lightly to his feet,
And went up into the white castle:
And when he was entered into the white castle,
Behold, two young Latins met him,   200
Each with a sharp sword in his hand.
Right so they ran upon Grujica,
That he stooped down to the black earth,
But with his untried sword he smote such buffets,
That of the two Latins he made four.
And as he went down out of the castle,
He was ware of the damsel Jerina.
"Tarry a little," quoth she, "youthful Grujica!"
And therewithal she threw him a golden apple.
"Take it," quoth she, "youthful Grujica,   210
That if ye should be in straits,
Ye may know where Jerina abideth!"
Grujica went down to Starina Novak,
Bearing with him the heads of the Latins.

Scarce had Grujica sat him down at the table,
When from the wall the Latin stripling called:
"Hear ye, kum Starina Novak!
Lo, down yonder under the white tower,
There be three valiant steeds,
To the saddles thereof are fixed three war-spears   220
Whose points are dressed upward to the sky;
If ye may leap over the three valiant steeds,
Then shall ye lead away the damsel Jerina."
When Starina Novak heard it,
He looked at Kraljević Marko,
Marko looked at Janko of Sibinj,
Janko looked at Bosnian Relja,
Relja leapt lightly to his feet,
And hied him under the white tower,
And lightly leaped over the three valiant steeds,   230
And the three war-spears that were dressed thereon.
Then he pulled out his good sabre,
For around the steeds were twelve knights on horseback,
And Relja slew them all twelve.
Then he took the three valiant steeds,
And led them to Starina Novak.
Scarce was Relja seated at the table,
When yet again the stripling shouted from the wall:
"Arise, thou kum, Starina Novak!
And shoot at the apple in the castle!"   240
Novak looked at Miloš the vojvoda,
Miloš leapt lightly to his feet,
He took his bow with the golden bowstring,
With an arrow he pierced the apple,
And bore it to Starina Novak.
Therewith Marko Kraljević waxed wroth,
And spake unto Starina Novak, saying:
"If I but knew where Jerina abideth,
I should have no more parley with these Latins."
Thereat up spake the youthful Grujica: 250
"Follow me, Kraljević Marko," said he,

"For I have seen where Jerina abideth."
They went up into the slender tower,
And found the damsel Jerina,
And led her down out of the slender tower.
With that the Latin stripling cried from the wall:
"Hearken ye, Starina Novak,
There be now closed against you
Seven and seventy gates."
Upon that Marko Kraljević spake a word: 260
"Grujica," quoth he, "bring me my charger Sharatz,
For on him are the keys of the gates."
And when Marko was mounted on Sharatz,
He drew his heavy mace,
And so did his anger rage,
That each door as he smote it,
Brast altogether in sunder,
Till he was come to the gate of the citadel,
A mighty gate it was, God's curse upon it!
And when Marko smote it with his heavy mace,   270
The whole castle shook to its foundations,
And stones fell down from the walls.
Upon that the King lift up his voice,
In Dubrovnik castle where the adventure was—
"Marko," saith he, "smite no more!"
Then he hasted and ran and brought the keys,
And opened the doors of the gate.
Marko stood by the doors of the gate,
And counted his thousand wedding-guests,
Till the tale was complete and they were gone forth
    every one.   280
Then said Marko to the King:
"Come hither, friend and king,
Come hither that we may give thee gifts,
And also that we may ask pardon
For any scathe that haply hath been done."
The King of Dubrovnik went to him,
For he thought and expected,

That Marko should give presents to him.
But Marko swung his heavy mace,
And the King fell dead in the gateway.   290
And the wedding-guests departed thence,
And came straight to Smederevo castle.
And when they were come to Smederevo castle,
Djuro gave them fair welcome,
And kept them for fifteen days.
Then Djuro went with Jerina into his castle,
And the others departed each to his own dwelling.

THE MARRIAGE OF STOJAN POPOVIĆ[1]

STOJAN POPOVIĆ wooed a maiden,
He wooed a maiden afar off,
In rich Latin Venice.
And she was daughter to Michael, King of Venice.
He put a ring on her finger and set a day for the wedding,
After he should have gone to his white manor,
And gathered the well-beseen wedding-guests.
And by the time he had given ring and apple,
He had spent three charges of gold;
In gifts also for mother-in-law and sister-in-law,   10
Stojan spended a thousand ducats.
And the King spake softly to Stojan:
"Son-in-law," quoth he, "Stojan Popović!
Gather thou wedding-guests as many as thou wilt,
And come for the damsel when good thee seemeth:
But hearken, Stojan Popović!
Bring not Serbs as thy wedding-guests,
For overmuch do the Serbs love drinking,
And of brawling also are they overfond,   19
They would get drunken, they would raise strife and tumult,
And it is ill to stay tumult
In sculptured[2] Venice of the Latins.
Bring with thee, therefore, Greeks and Bulgars."
When the Lady Queen heard these words,
She cast a glance at Stojan,
At Stojan she cast a glance and a smile.
And now Stojan made him ready,
And went forth of the white palace.
And on the road a letter came to him,
From his mother-in-law, the damsel's mother: 30

[1] "Concerning this Stojan Popović, I have never heard anything more, nor do I know anything more than what is here given" (Vuk).

[2] Плетеноме вала да значи оно, што је по кућама спола у камену изрезано којешта. (Vuk's note.)

"Son-in-law," saith she, "Stojan Popović!
Bring with thee nor Greeks nor Bulgars;
Ask none save Serbs only to be thy wedding-guests,
For the Latins were ever deceivers,
And of some treason thou mayst be well adread."
When this letter came to Stojan,
He fell on thinking,
And in this study drew nigh to his manor.
Right so his mother came forth to meet him,
And they halsed and kissed each the other,   40
And Stojan kissed his mother's hand.
Then Stojan's mother asked him:
"Say now, my son Stojan,
Art thou come to me in peace?
Hast thou won for me a daughter,
For me a daughter, for thyself a faithful wife?"
Stojan Popović made answer:
"In peace am I come, mother,
And I have won a daughter for thee,
For thee a daughter, for myself a faithful wife.   50
Three charges of gold have I spended,
Forby a thousand ducats,
For gifts for mother-in-law and sister-in-law:
And the King spake to me to this end,
That I should bring no Serbs as wedding-guests,
But only Greeks and Bulgars.
And on the way hither, mother,
A letter overtook me from the maid's mother,
Bidding me bring Serbs as wedding-guests.
Rede me now, mother,   60
Whether of these counsels were better to follow?"
Stojan's mother made answer:
"It were better, my son, to obey the maid's mother,
For the Latins were ever deceivers.
As kum take the King of Buda,
As stari svat Vuk Mandušić,
As vojvoda, Janko of Sibinj,

As čauš, the wingéd Relja,
As barjaktar, Miloš Obilić,
As dever, Kraljević Marko,   70
And others as good thee seemeth.
So shalt thou fear no treason."
Stojan hearkened to his mother's counsel;
He sent out letters everywhither,
For to gather the well-beseen wedding-guests.
And he gathered a thousand wedding-guests.
The kum was the King of Buda,
The stari svat was Vuk Mandušić,
The vojvoda was Janko of Sibinj,
The čauš was the wingéd Relja,   80
The barjaktar was Miloš Obilić,
And the dever was Marko Kraljević.
So they set out for Latin Venice,
And when they were come to Latin Venice,
The King gave them fair welcome,
The horses were led down to the stables,
And the knights were brought into the white castle.
When the morning of the fourth day dawned,
The gay-clad čauš cried aloud:
"Hazurala! Arise, ye wedding-guests!   90
The days are short and long are the stages,
The hour is come that we must depart hence."
Right on that the King of Venice came forth,
Bringing lordly presents.
To the kum he gave a shirt of gold,
To the stari svat a golden tray,
To the vojvoda a golden apple,
To the čauš he gave a spear,
To Miloš a rich-chased sabre,
To Kraljević he gave a heavy mace.   100
He gave him also the bride and the horse whereon she
     rode.
"Lo, Marko, horse and maid are in thy keeping,
Till ye be come to Stojan's manor,

And there thou shalt give over to him the fair damsel."
With that the wedding-guests arose,
And bravely did the King conduct them forth,
To all the wedding-guests he gave gifts in turn,
To one a kerchief, to another a shirt all rare embroidered.
So they departed thence in merry wise,
And gat them up into the mountain.   110
And when they were come up into the mountain,
There sat a knight by the highway,
That was clad right marvellously,
All in silver and in fine gold.
His mighty plumes came down over him,
Yea, brothers, down to the green grass!
Black indeed was his moustache about his teeth,
And in size it was as large as a lamb of half a year.
Through his moustache a breastplate shone,
Like the bright sun through woodland trees.   120
His legs were yellow to the knee,
Yea, my brothers, with purest gold!
His mace was hard by him,
In his lap lay his battle-spear,
On his thigh was a rich-wrought sabre.
And ever as the knight drank the red wine,
The Vila of the mountain served him;
With her right hand she gave him to drink from a
          golden cup,
And with her left she gave him to eat.
Now when the wedding-guests should have passed by,   130
The knight leapt lightly to his feet,
And spake to the King of Buda:
"Ha, Sir King!" quoth he,
"Ha, Sir Kum! Throw down the golden shirt
That they gave thee yonder."
The King yielded it without a word.
The King passed on and Vuk drew nigh,
And of him the knight required the golden tray,
And Vuk gave it without a word.

Then came Janko of Sibinj,   140
Of him was required the golden apple,
And Janko gave it without a word.
Next came the wingéd Relja,
Forthwith the knight required his spear of him,
And Relja gave it without a word.
Then Miloš of Pocerje drew near,
But when the knight required of him his rich-wrought
     sabre,
Fain would Miloš have had ado with him,
But his fellows cried out upon him, saying:
"Give up thy sabre, seek not to do battle!"   150
And Miloš yielded up the rich-wrought sabre.
And behold Marko Kraljević cometh,
With the damsel on horseback with him.
Forthwithal the knight lift up his voice:
"Ha, Sir Marko!" quoth he,
"Give me now the horse and the damsel,
That they gave to thee down yonder."
Kraljević Marko made answer:
"Brother-in-God, thou Latin giant,
The horse is not mine, and the maid is another's,   160
Yet soothly, brother, they gave me a present,
A gift for mine own self—a heavy mace—
The which I am well minded to give thee."
The giant would not answer him again,
But he sought to seize the horse
Whereon the damsel sat.
So Marko drew his heavy mace,
By quickness he deceived the eyes of the Latin,
Then he swung mightily with his mace,
And smote the Latin between his dark eyes,   170
That both eyes sprang forth of his head.
Then went Marko Kraljević to him,
And cut off the giant's head;
He stripped from off him his fair gear,
And he took also the lordly presents,

And gave them back to the wedding-guests.
To the kum he gave the golden shirt,
To the stari svat the golden tray,
To the vojvoda the golden apple,
To the čauš he gave back the spear,   180
To Miloš the rich-wrought sabre,
And to Marko remained the heavy mace.
So the guests continued on their way,
Marko went up the mountain singing,
The giant tarried in the throes of death[1].

[1] Оста цине ногом копајући: this is the same expression as is
used to describe the end of Philip the Magyar.

THE DEATH OF MARKO KRALJEVIĆ

Marko Kraljević rode forth early,
On a Sabbath morn before the bright sun,
He rode by the sea shore towards Urvina mountain.
And when Marko was gone up into the mountain,
Behold Sharatz began to stumble,
To stumble, yea, and to shed tears.
Thereat Marko was much grieved,
And he said unto Sharatz:
"What aileth thee, Sharo? What aileth thee, my good steed?
An hundred and sixty years have we been together,   10
And never or now hath thy foot failed thee,
But today thou stumblest,
God wot, this bodeth no good thing.
One of us twain will surely lose his head,
Or my head or haply thine."
Thus Marko was discoursing,
When the Vila cried from Urvina mountain,
And called to Kraljević Marko:
"Brother-in-God, Kraljević Marko!
Wouldst thou know, brother, wherefore thy horse
    stumbleth?   20
Sharatz is heavy for thee, his master,
For soon shall ye be divided."
But Marko answered the Vila:
"White Vila," quoth he, "a plague on thy tongue!
Since that with him I have seen the earth and the cities
    thereof,
And am gone to and fro from the east unto the west,
Nor found nowhere better horse than Sharatz,
Nor never knight that put me to the worse,
I think not to separate me from Sharatz,
Whilst my head endureth on my shoulders."   30
But the white Vila answered him again,

"Brother-in-God, Kraljević Marko!
Truly none may take Sharatz from thee,
Nor mayst thou be slain, Marko,
By means of might or by sharp sword,
By war-spear or by battle-mace.
Thou fearest no earthly knight,
Yet shalt thou die, Marko,
By the hand of God, that old slayer.
But if thou wilt not believe me,   40
When thou comest to the top of the mountain,
Look about thee from the right hand to the left,
And thou shalt see two slim fir trees
That out-top all the trees of the forest,
And crown the forest with their verdure,
And between them is a well of water;
Do thou ride Sharatz thither,
Light down from him and tie him to a fir tree,
Then bend thee down over the well of water,
And thou shalt see thy face mirrored,   50
And thou shalt know when thou must die."
Marko hearkened unto the Vila,
And when he was come to the top of the mountain,
He looked about him from the right hand unto the left,
And he was ware of two slender fir trees
That out-topped all the trees of the forest,
And crowned it with their verdure.
Thither he steered Sharatz,
And lighting down tied him to a fir tree.
Then he stooped him down over the well of water, 60
And considered his countenance in the water;
And when he had considered his countenance,
He wist well when he should die,
And he shed tears and spake on this wise:
"Deceitful world—thou wert a fair flower to me!
Fair wert thou, but few the years of my sojourn.
Three hundred brief years have I tarried;
The hour now cometh that I must go forth of this world."

Then Marko pulled out his sabre,
From his girdle he pulled out his sabre,   70
He came nigh unto his horse Sharatz,
And with his sabre cut off the head of Sharatz,
That never he should fall into the hands of the Turks,
Nor never be for a slave to them,
Nor bear for them the copper water-pots.
And when Marko had slain Sharatz,
He buried his horse Sharatz,
He buried Sharatz better than he had buried Andrew
     his brother.
In four pieces he broke his sharp sabre,
Lest the Turks, finding it,   80
Should boast them to have gotten it of Marko,
And so cause Christians to revile him.
And after Marko had broken his sharp sabre,
He brake his war-spear in seven pieces,
And cast them into the fir branches.
Then Marko took his ribbed mace,
In his right hand he took it,
And cast it from Urvina mountain
Into the great grey sea;
And concerning the mace he spake, saying: 90
"When my mace shall come up out of the sea,
Another Marko shall appear upon earth!"
And when he had destroyed his weapons,
He drew forth an inkhorn from his girdle,
From his pocket he took unwritten paper,
And therewithal he wrote a letter:
"Whoso cometh up into Urvina mountain,
Unto the well between the fir trees,
And findeth there the knight Marko,
Let him wit well that Marko is dead,   100
And by Marko there be three purses of gold[1],
Yea, verily of gold, of yellow ducats;
One purse I give to him that findeth me,

    [1] Lit. "three money-belts."

That he may bury my body;
Another purse I give for to adorn the churches,
The third I give to the maimed and the blind,
That the blind may go into all the world,
To sing and to celebrate Marko."
When Marko had made an end of writing,
He fixed the letter on a branch of the fir tree,   110
Where one might see it from the road.
He cast his golden inkhorn into the well,
He did off his green mantle,
And spread it on the grass beneath the fir trees,
He made the sign of the rood and sate him down on the
      mantle;
He pulled his sable kalpak over his eyes,
Then laid him down never to rise no more.
By the well lay the dead Marko,
From day and again to day, a week of days,
For whoso by adventure passed that way   120
And was ware of Marko,
He did think ever that Marko surely slept,
And made wide his path round about him,
For fear lest he should wake Marko.
Where good fortune is, there also is evil fortune,
And where evil fortune is, there is good fortune also;
And truly good fortune it was,
That led thither Vaso the Igumen
From white Vilindar church on the Holy Mountain,
With Isaias, his deacon, with him.   130
And when the Igumen was ware of Marko,
With his right hand he beckoned the deacon:
"Softly, my son," quoth he, "lest thou wake him,
For Marko roused from slumber is evil-disposed,
And might well make an end of both of us."
But as the monk looked to see how Marko slept,
He perceived the letter above him,
And heedfully he read it,
And the letter told him that Marko was dead.

Right on that the monk lighted down from his horse,　140
And touched with his hand the worshipful Marko,
But Marko was already long dead.
Vaso, the Igumen, wept tears,
For he was passing heavy because of Marko.
From his girdle he took the three purses of gold,
And girded them about his own middle.
Then Vaso, the Igumen, thought and considered
Where he should bury the dead Marko;
He thought and considered and took resolve,
And he set the dead Marko upon his horse,　150
And so brought him to the sea-shore.
He sate him down in a ship with the dead Marko
　　with him,
And brought him with a straight course to the Holy
　　Mountain
And so to the church of Vilindar.
And he let carry him into the church of Vilindar,
Over Marko he read words meet for the dead,
And in the earth he buried his body,
In the middle church of white Vilindar.
There the old man buried Marko,
But he left no sign thereon,　160
That none should know the grave of Marko,
And that his enemies should not revenge them on
　　the dead.

APPENDIX

THE DATE OF THE BALLADS

OF the court poetry that is said to have flourished in the time of Tsar Dushan and before it, nothing has come down to us, and after Kossovo (1389) anything in the nature of court poetry must speedily have ceased to exist. But Serbian minstrelsy did not altogether perish; the popular ballad gained new force and significance, and in all probability the heroes of Kossovo were already widely sung during the life-time of many who had actually fought in that battle. For the Serb is a born maker, and the two Greek historians Ducas and Laonicas, who are thought to have lived within seventy-five years of the date of Kossovo, are both familiar with the traditional story of the struggle. Laonicas, indeed, relates how a Serbian knight called Μήλοις rode alone into the Turkish camp. Pretending to be a deserter with important information he gained access to Murad's presence and slew the Sultan with a spear-thrust. Ducas tells much the same story but does not give the name of the Serbian knight; he says, moreover, that the weapon used was a dagger, on which point he is in agreement with the existing poems.

An anonymous translation of Ducas in Italian contains many additional details that are certainly drawn from poems, quite in the manner of Pitscottie's "Chronicle," and as this Italian version dates from the fifteenth century, it is clear that Murad's death at the hands of Miloš had become a well-known ballad theme very soon indeed after the event[1].

But the earliest direct references to the poems are in German, and occur in the writings of Kuripešić who travelled from Vienna to Constantinople in 1531[2].

Stephan Gerlach relates in his diary (1573–78) that near Pirot the ruins of a castle were pointed out to him as being once the abode of Miloš Obilić: "Die Christen sagen, das Milosch Coboli, welcher den türkischen Kayser Murat erstochen, da seine Wohnung gehabt habe." With reference to dancing and the singing of folk-songs he says: "Nach dem Essen haben die Jungfern in einem Reyhen getantzt und Chorweise gesungen, je zwei und zwei miteinander...[3]."

With regard to the Marko ballads, the oldest known (a pesme dugog

[1] Chadwick, *The Heroic Age*, pp. 313–316; Knolles, *Generall Historie of the Turkes*, p. 200 (ed. 1620); Gibbon, VII. p. 327.
[2] Ćurčin, *Das serbische Volkslied*, p. 15; Ranke, *History of Servia*, p. 53 footnote. Kuripešić mentions Obilić as a hero of popular song.
[3] Ćurčin, p. 15, from Prof. V. Jagić's *Material zur Geschichte der slavischen Volkspoesie*. I. *Historische Zeugnisse*. Zagreb, 1876, p. 83 ff.

stiha) occurs in the *"Ribanje"* of Petar Hektorović (1556)[1], but the earliest date that can be assigned to the poems in their decasyllabic form is the seventeenth century[2].

VUK

Vuk Stefanović Karadžić (1787–1864) was born at Tršić of well-to-do peasant folk. His father's name was Stefan Joksimović and, following the Serb custom, the son bore the surname of Stefanović— Stefan's son. His parents had already lost several children so, as a measure of precaution, they bestowed on the boy the "prezime" of Vuk, a name supposed to be potent against the charms of witches and the Evil Eye[3]. Vuk's childhood was spent with his peasant parents and he was thus familiar from the first with the life of the country folk. It was a primitive life, for conditions had remained unchanged since the Turkish conquest of the fifteenth century. The Turk, indeed, had played the part of wicked fairy, and in Serbia all cultural progress had been arrested as completely as in the palace of the Sleeping Beauty.

Neither of Vuk's parents could read, but the boy contrived to learn somehow, and his father sent him to the monastery of Tronoša in the hope that he might be able to further his studies there, but the experiment was not a success, the monks were entirely absorbed in the cultivation of their fields, and Vuk returned home to tend cattle.

While thus employed, he made ink for himself by dissolving gunpowder in water, and began to write down local songs and proverbs. This was the modest beginning of the great collections of folk-song with which his name is associated. In 1804, the year of the Serbian rising under Karageorge, Vuk took service with one of the patriot leaders. The Turks advanced, Tršić was burned to the ground, and Vuk's chief was killed.

For some years thereafter Vuk led a wandering life. We hear of him at Karlovatz gymnasium, at various places in Serbia, and finally at Belgrade where, as the result of a serious illness, he became permanently lame. "Upheld by crutches," he writes, "I could think no more of war and horses, yet had it not been for these same crutches I had surely been slain by the Turks, like so many of my contemporaries. Thanks to my crutches I had, perforce, to stay at home, and there I set down on paper what my ears had heard and what my eyes had seen." In 1813, when Karageorge made his escape over the Danube, Vuk fled also and settled in Vienna. At this time the remarkable body of Serbian songs and ballads which we now possess had not yet been committed to writing

[1] The poem describes a quarrel between Marko and Andrija. It begins : Dva mi sta siromaka dugo vreme drugovala. In a report from Spalato to the Venetian Senate in 1547 it is stated that *"*a blind soldier sang a song about Marko Kraljević and everybody joined in for everybody knew it." Dr Branko Vodnik, *Narodne pjesme hrvatsko-srpske.* Zagreb, 1918.

[2] Prof. Popović, *Jugoslovenska Književnost*, pp. 57 and 65.

[3] See p. 78 note. The word "Vuk" means "wolf."

but was still at the stage of oral tradition. Such written and printed matter as did exist was almost entirely of a religious or official nature, and was composed in the Paleo-Slav of the Church, an archaic language unintelligible to the people. The original alphabet of Cyril[1] the Byzantine missionary of the ninth century had become quite unsuitable as a means of expressing the sounds of the spoken language, and when Kopitar urged upon Vuk the importance of publishing his collected material it became clear that the first necessity was to reform the ancient Cyrillic alphabet so as to adapt it to the needs of the living tongue. Vuk undertook the task and carried it through with triumphant success in spite of the bitterest clerical opposition, and to-day the Serbs, alone in Europe, enjoy the privilege of possessing a true phonetic alphabet. With the publication of the Grammar and of the first collection of Serbian folk-songs in 1814, Vuk may be said to have found his vocation.

Advised and assisted by Kopitar, he produced after several years of laborious work his great Serbian Dictionary, a book which was received by scholars with the liveliest satisfaction. Learned societies began to honour him and in 1820, on the invitation of Prince Milosh, he returned to Belgrade to help in the task of establishing a system of national education. But those who regarded, or professed to regard, the reform of the alphabet as an act of sacrilege, were so strong and bitter in their hostility, that Vuk was compelled to leave. He returned to Vienna and prepared another collection of folk-songs for the press. Here again difficulty beset him, and obstacles were placed in the way of publication. Vuk, accordingly, travelled to Leipzig in 1823 and had the book printed there (1823). He became the personal friend of Goethe, Jacob Grimm, Humboldt, Ranke and many other distinguished men, but their generous appreciation did not save him from the pinch of downright poverty.

"I cannot tell you," he wrote to a friend, "in what difficulties I find myself. Believe me, I was unable to buy a pound of meat, far less a pig, for Christmas. Remembering what day it was, and looking at my children, I wept like a child. Everything I can sell or pawn, I have sold or pawned, and now I know not what I am to do with my wife and children. It is winter, and I have no wood, no bread and no money."

Gradually, however, his circumstances improved and a pension was granted him. The remainder of his life was largely spent in travel in Serbia, Bosnia and Montenegro, and in the publication of the material thus collected.

---

[1] Constantine, who changed his name to Cyril on being ordained bishop by Pope Hadrian II, devised the alphabet known as the *glagolitic* alphabet about the year 863. The alphabet now universally called by his name was framed half a century later by another hand. It was a distinct improvement, but it was based on Cyril's work, and Cyril's name has become indissolubly associated with this later alphabet of which he himself was not the author.

"He was of medium height," says a contemporary, "his face, with its high cheek-bones, looked curiously triangular and his small, deep-set, twinkling blue eyes were almost always downcast. He had bushy grey eyebrows and a huge moustache: he habitually wore high boots and a long black coat: his left leg was shorter than the right, for which reason he was unable to move about without a crutch: on his head he wore a large red fez which he very seldom removed."

Respected and honoured by the literary and scientific world as no Serbian had been before him, he lived long enough to see the complete victory of the reforms for which he had fought, and to the last he pursued his strenuous labours, in order, as he said, "to snatch something more from death."

Vuk died and was buried in Vienna in 1864, but thirty years later his remains were transferred to his native land and re-interred with great pomp near the west door of the cathedral in Belgrade[1].

MARKO KRALJEVIĆ

(Vuk's article in the *Rječnik*.)

There is no Serb to whom the name of Marko Kraljević is unfamiliar. I propose to mention here certain incidents in his career which, for the greater part, are not in the heroic ballads, but occur in tales and legends. Marko is reputed to have been much stronger than any man living, either then or now. In the 71st ballad of the 2nd book[2] ("The Turks at Marko's Slava"), Marko's mace, which he swung and flung with one hand, is said to have weighed 66 okas[3].

As a boy I saw a painting of Marko in the hospice of the monastery at Krušedol in Syrmia. He was depicted carrying a full-grown ox by the tail. He had slung the animal over his shoulder and strode along without bending beneath the burden. In ballad No. 66 ("Marko Kraljević and Musa Kesedžija"), the story is told of how he took in his hand a piece of dry cornel-wood "from a rafter ten years old," and how when he crushed it in his grasp it broke "in two pieces and in three," and two drops of water came forth out of it. Marko could not go anywhere without ample provision of wine, but as his strength was great, so great was his power of drinking without getting drunk.

With regard to Šarac, some say that a Vila made Marko a present of him; others assert that Marko bought him from certain pack-horse drivers[4]. They say he had made trial of many horses before Šarac, but

[1] Mr Alexander Yovitchitch was present at the exhumation. When the coffin was opened Vuk was revealed, fez on head, looking like one who slept.

[2] Српске Народне Пјесме: Книга друга. Свеска 2. (Belgrade, 1895.) Also in the later edition of 1913.

[3] The oka = 1·280 kilos. Marko's mace, accordingly, weighed 186 lbs.

[4] Кирициja: a kind of hawker who used to carry his own or his master's goods from town to town on a pack-horse or in a light cart.

that not one of them was able to carry him. One day he saw a piebald, leprous foal among the pack-horses belonging to some carriers, and it seemed to him that the animal had the makings of a fine steed. Forthwith he seized him by the tail in order to swing him round, as he had done with all the other horses he had hitherto tested, but he failed to move this horse from the place where he stood. Thereupon he bought Šarac from his owner, cured him of his leprosy, and taught him to drink wine. Of the death of Marko Kraljević various stories are told. Some say he fell at the village of Rovina in a battle between Turks and Vlachs. He was slain, they say, by a Wallachian chief called Mirčeta who shot him in the mouth with a golden arrow. Others say that in the course of the battle Šarac was engulfed in a swamp near the Danube, and that both horse and rider perished there.

In the Negotin district the story goes that the event took place in a morass in the neighbourhood, not far from the Caričina spring (Königinbrunn). The morass is still there, and the ruins of an old church, said to have been built over Marko's grave, are still standing. According to another legend, so many perished in the battle of Rovina that horses and horsemen began to swim in blood, whereupon Marko, raising his hands to heaven, cried out: "O God, what shall I do now?" God took pity on him and miraculously transported Šarac and his master to a cave where both continue to live to this day. Thrusting his sword into the rock, Marko lay down and fell asleep and still he sleeps. Before Šarac is a patch of moss at which he nibbles from time to time. Little by little Marko's sword emerges from the rock, and when Šarac eats all the moss and the sword falls down at last out of the rock, then shall Marko once more go forth into the world. Another story is that he fled to the cave after seeing a musket for the first time. Beginning to experiment with it he shot himself through the hand[1]. Whereupon he said: "Henceforth valour is of no avail, for now the meanest wretch may slay the bravest knight."

MARRIAGE

An immense mass of traditional observances centres round the act of marriage even in a place like Belgrade, where the ceremony is shorn of many interesting details still to be found in the country districts. As in France, it is the rule that the parents should arrange the marriage of their children and this is done by means of a provodadžija or intermediary. Sometimes a regular deputation goes to the house of the bride bearing an apple—the symbol of fertility. There is a deal of vague talk between the parties before the real business of the hour is broached, but of course everybody knows beforehand what is coming. At last the apple is laid on the table, the girl is summoned, and when she takes

[1] One gathers that he did this intentionally in order to find out what the weapon was capable of.

it, as she always does, the "suitor" produces rakija—the просачка буклија mentioned on p. 38, line 334—and the bargain is sealed.

A full-dress Serbian wedding is an imposing affair, and it may be well to state very briefly the names and functions of the chief personages in the cavalcade. They are catalogued in the two ballads entitled "The Marriage of Djuro of Smederevo," p. 159, and in "The Marriage of Stojan Popović," p. 168.

> *Kum:* 1st witness, sponsor or godfather; the chief personage from the religious point of view. The relationship between the kum and the bridal pair is considered one of the most sacred and binding. A fictitious blood-relationship is established which precludes inter-marriage between the respective families in perpetuity[1].

> Three kinds of kumstvo are commonly recognised:

> (1) Kršteno kumstvo = sponsorship at baptism.
> (2) Kumstvo vjenčano = „ marriage.
> (3) Kumstvo šišano = „ the hair-cutting.

> *Dever:* the bride-leader (παράνυμφος). Sometimes there are two *deveri.* They are the bridegroom's most trusted friends. Cf. Gk. δαήρ, Lat. levir.

> *Stari svat:* "the senior wedding-guest"; the 2nd witness. On the wedding-day he stands behind the bride and it is he who acts as M.C. at the wedding feast.

> *Čauš:* in the ballads the čauš appears to mean a kind of marshaller of the wedding-cavalcade. The word comes from the Turkish and signifies literally "a herald." Nowadays it is applied to the licensed jester whose duty it is to bandy witticisms with all and sundry and so keep the guests amused.

> *Vojvoda:* the leader of the procession; very often the bridegroom's uncle.

> *Barjaktar:* the standard-bearer.

> *Privenac:* "nuptialium hominum quidam," says Vuk. He suggests that the word may be a corruption of prvijenac.

> *Prikumak:* the kum's attendant; he sometimes acts as barjaktar also.

THE "SLAVA" OR "KRSNO IME"

Every Serb family has a patron saint whose ikon hangs in a conspicuous place in the house and each year, when the saint's day comes round, the family holds a celebration known as the "Slava" or "Krsno ime."

It is a social duty to call on one's friends on the day they hold their Slava, and I have before me a sort of Slava directory published in Belgrade for the convenience of the inhabitants. This little book is entitled "Имена Свечара" and contains a list of saints' days with the dates on which they fall[2]. Under the name of each saint are

---

[1] Cf. Sir Henry Maine, *Early Law and Custom*, pp. 257–259.

[2] This list of Slava days and the families celebrating them was compiled in 1896.

printed the names of the families which celebrate their Slava on that particular day. Thirty-eight different saints are enumerated and inspection of the list shows that:

On St John's Day (Свети Јован, Jan. 7 O.S.), 361 families celebrate.
On St George's Day (Ђурђевдан, April 23), 252 families celebrate.
On St Michael's Day (Св. Архангел Михаило, Nov. 8), 414 families celebrate.
On St Nicholas' Day (Св. Никола, Dec. 6), 699 families celebrate.

The above are the most popular dates. On St Barbara's Day, on the other hand (Dec. 4), only one family, that of Живко Петровић, is given as celebrating its Slava. "Slava" literally means "glory" and is the word used in the Bible as a rendering of "hosanna." There is also the verbal form "slaviti" to celebrate or glorify, the use of which is illustrated in the lines:

> Већ ме пусти, царе поочиме,
> Да прославим моје крсно име.
> ("Marko Kraljević and Mina of Kostura," ll. 103–104.)

Krsno ime = the baptismal name—an expression used as an alternative to Slava.

The commonly accepted account of the origin of the custom is as follows. Before the missionaries from Byzantium and Rome had converted the Serbs to Christianity, the latter had a native cult of the household deity corresponding to the Latin cult of the Penates. As each family or clan was baptized into the new faith, the baptismal day was associated by the priest with the name of some convenient saint whose ikon, displayed in the house, took the place of the old pagan Hausgeist in the religious life of the family[1]. But the matter is, in reality, not quite so simple. The Serbs were converted in the ninth century and there appears to be no mention of the Krsno ime prior to the fourteenth century. Another difficulty is that the Slava is not observed either by the Croats or the Bulgars, and, although we may guess at possible explanations, the fact remains that materials are lacking on which a reliable account of the development of this interesting custom might be based[2].

The Slava has been repeatedly described in English, and there is no need to go over the ground in detail here[3]. The priest blesses the house and sprinkles each room with holy water. He then holds a service with the family before the ikon and its lighted candle. The kolač—a flat

[1] Krauss, *Sitte und Brauch der Südslaven*, pp. 51–57.
[2] Jireček, *Geschichte der Serben*, pp. 180–181.
[3] *E.g.*, Mijatovich, *Servia and the Servians*; Lazarovich-Hrebelianovich, *The Servian People*, vol. I. pp. 56–62; W. M. Petrovitch, *Hero-tales and Legends of the Serbians*, p. 40 ff.

circular cake of wheaten flour bearing the letters $\left(\begin{array}{c|c} \text{НС} & \text{ХР} \\ \hline \text{НН} & \text{КА} \end{array}\right)$ embossed
within the arms of a cross—is bent slightly by the *svečar*[1] and the
priest so as to break open the surface of the cake along the lines of
the cross when the priest pours in a few drops of red wine. On one
occasion, when I was privileged to assist at the private family service,
the *svečar* was perturbed to discover, just before the priest arrived,
that there was white wine only in the house. The priest entered and on
learning how matters stood he said sternly: "Christ's blood was red,"
and refused to proceed with the service until a bottle of red wine had
been sent for[2]. In addition to the *kolač*, another cake, made of boiled
wheat, dusted over with white powdered sugar—the *koljivo*—plays
an essential part in the ceremony. The word is said to mean "something
killed with the knife[3]," and is supposed by some to be the Christian
substitute for actual sacrifice. Certainly it is significant that the *koljivo*
is used not only at the Slava but also at the feasts for the dead—the
daća. Moreover on the days dedicated to Saint Elias (July 20, O.S.)
and to the Archangel Michael (Nov. 8), the Slava is celebrated *without*
the *koljivo*, the explanation being that neither St Elias nor St Michael
has ever died and therefore the offering to the souls of the dead sym-
bolised by the *koliivo* would here be inappropriate.

[1] Svečar = the head of the household where the Slava is being held.
[2] In Belgrade on St Nicholas' Day, 1907.
[3] Cf. Petrovitch's account, p. 41.

BIBLIOGRAPHY

ALBERTO FORTIS. Saggio d'Osservazioni sopra l'isola di Cherso ed Osero. (Venice, 1771.)
—— Viaggio in Dalmazia. 2 vols. (Venice, 1774.)
—— Travels into Dalmatia. (London, 1778.)
—— Die Sitten der Morlacken. (Bern, 1775.)
—— Abbate Alberto Fortis Reise in Dalmatien. (Bern, 1776.)
—— Voyage en Dalmatie. (Berne, 1788.)
ANDRIJA KAČIĆ MIOŠIĆ. Razgovor ugodni naroda slovinskoga. (First known edition published at Venice, 1756.)
J. F. HERDER. Ein Gesang von Milos Cobilich und Vuko Brankovich. Morlakisch. ("Volkslieder," Erster Teil. Leipzig, 1778.)
—— Radoslaus. Eine Morlakische Geschichte.
—— Die schöne Dolmetscherin. Eine Morlakische Geschichte. ("Volkslieder," Zweiter Teil. Leipzig, 1779.)
These three translations of Herder's are to be found in vol. xxv of the "Sämtliche Werke."
J. W. V. GOETHE. Klaggesang von der edlen Frauen des Asan Aga…Aus dem Morlackischen. (First published in Herder's "Volkslieder" in 1778.) Vol. I. pp. 151–153 of the Cotta edition.
—— Über Kunst und Alterthum, vols. v and vi, 1825, 1827. (Here are essays and reviews dealing with the Serbian folk-song. All are to be found in vol. xxix of Hempel's edition.)
VUK STEFANOVIĆ KARADŽIĆ. Mala prostonarodnja slavenoserbska pjesnarića. Izdana Vukom Stefanovićem. (Vienna Narodna srbska pjesnarica. Cast utora. Vienna, 1815.)
—— Narodne srpske pjesme. Skupio i na svijet izdao Vuk Stef. Karadžić. Knjiga prva, u kojoj su različne ženske pjesme. (Leipzig: Breitkopf u. Härtel, 1825.)
—— Narodne srpske pjesme, vol. II (Leipzig, 1823); vol. III (Leipzig, 1823); vol. IV (Vienna, 1823).
A new and very greatly enlarged edition was published in Vienna between the years 1841–1862. This was followed by the Belgrade edition which was begun in 1887 and completed in 1896. Vol. II, containing the Marko cycle and many other epic ballads, has been reprinted several times.
—— Grammar of the Serbian tongue. (Pismenica serbskoga jezika. Vienna, 1814.)
Jacob Grimm wrote a German translation of this Grammar. (Leipzig and Berlin, 1824.) He contributed also an admirable "Vorrede" which is reprinted in the "Kleinere Schriften," vol. VIII. pp. 96–129.

Vuk Stefanovic Karadžić. Srpski Rječnik—Lexicon serbico-ger-
manico-latinum. (Vienna, 1818.) My own copy is the Belgrade
edition, 1898. It is a treasure-house of information and an indis-
pensable aid to the student.
—— Srpske Narodne Pripovijetke. (Belgrade, 1897.)
—— Život i običaji naroda srpskoga. (Wien, 1867.)
Jacob Grimm. Translations of nineteen Serbian songs in Förster's
"Sängerfahrt." (Berlin, 1818.) Reprinted in the "Kleinere
Schriften," iv. pp. 455–467.
—— Translation of the epic poem "Erbschaftsteilung" in "Kunst
und Alterthum," iv. (1824). Reprinted in "Kleinere Schriften,"
i. p. 410.
—— Die Aufbauung Scutaris. Grimm made two translations of this
poem, the first unmetrical, the second metrical. "Kleinere
Schriften," vii. pp. 544–555. Particularly useful is the "Vorrede"
to Grimm's German version of Vuk's "Grammar" (1824).
Reprinted in "Kleinere Schriften," viii. pp. 96–129.
Talvj (Therese Albertine Luise von Jacob. Afterwards Mrs Robinson).
Volkslieder der Serben. 2 vols. (Halle, 1825 and 1826.) 2nd
edition unchanged. (Halle and Leipzig, 1835.) New edition
revised and enlarged. 2 vols. (Leipzig, 1853.)
—— Historical View of the Languages and Literature of the Slavic
Nations: with a sketch of their popular poetry, by Talvj. With
a preface by Edward Robinson, D.D., LL.D., author of "Biblical
Researches in Palestine," etc. (New York: George P. Putnam,
1850.)
E. Eugen Wesely. Serbische Hochzeitslieder. (Pest, 1826.)
Westminster Review, vol. vi. 1826. Narodne Srpske Pjesme, 1823–4.
Popular Servian Songs, collected and published by Vuk Stephano-
vich Karatzich. (Leipzig, 3 vols. 8vo.)
John Bowring. Servian Popular Poetry. (London, 1827.)
Wilhelm Gerhard. Wila: Serbische Volkslieder und Helden-
märchen. 2 vols. (Leipzig, 1828.) A second edition of this work
was published at Leipzig in 1877, under the title of "Wilhelm
Gerhards Gesänge der Serben."
Johann Nepomuk Vogl. Marko Kraljevits—Serbische Heldensage.
(Vienna, 1851.)
Siegfried Kapper. Südslavische Wanderungen. 2 vols. (Leipzig,
1851.) The 1st vol. contains a sketch of our hero—"Marko, der
Königssohn. Eine Gestalt aus den serbischen Heldengesängen."
—— Die Gesänge der Serben. 2 vols. (Leipzig, 1852.)
Ludwig August Frankl. Gusle, Serbische Nationallieder. (Vienna,
1852.)
Leopold v. Ranke. History of Servia, pp. 47–56. A brief statement of
the significance of the national poetry. Marko receives special
attention. (English edition, Bohn, 1853.)

Owen Meredith. Serbski Pesme or National Songs of Servia. (London: Chapman and Hall, 1861.)

Carl Gröber. Der Königssohn Marko. (Vienna: Alfred Holder, 1883.) This book contains thirty-one ballads of which sixteen are to be found in Vuk.

Archiv für slavische Philologie:
Prof. V. Jagić. "Kraljević Marko kurz skizziert nach der serbischen Volksdichtung," v. pp. 439–455.
—— "Die südslavische Volksepik vor Jahrhunderten," iv. p. 192 f.

Stojan Novaković. "Ein Beitrag zur Literatur der serbischen Volkspoesie," iii. p. 640 ff.

A. Soerensen. "Beitrag zur Geschichte der Entwickelung der serbischen Heldendichtung," xiv, xv, xvi, xvii and xx. Continued as a separate publication under title of "Entstehung der kurzzeiligen serbo-kroatischen Liederdichtung in Küstenlande." (Weidmann, 1895.)

Gjorgje Popović. Turski i drugi istočanska reči u našem jeziku. (Belgrade, 1884.)

F. Miklošić. Die Türkischen Elemente in den Südost- und Osteuropäischen Sprachen. (Wien, 1888.)

M. G. Khalanski. Kraljević Marko. (In two parts. Warsaw, 1893–1894.)

Auguste Dozon. Poésies populaires serbes. (Paris, 1859.)
—— L'épopée serbe—chants populaires héroïques. (Paris, 1888.)

Louis Leger. La mythologie slave. (Paris, 1901.)
—— Le cycle épique de Marko Kraljević. (Journal des Savants. Paris, 1905.)
—— Le rénovateur de la littérature serbe: Vouk Stefanovitch Karadjitch. (Bibliothèque Universelle et Revue Suisse. Lausanne, 1921.)

Madame E. L. Mijatovich. Serbian Folk-Lore. Introduction by Rev. W. Denton. (London, 1874; 2nd ed. 1899.)
—— Kossovo. (London, 1881.)

Lazarovich-Hrebelianovich. The Servian People—Their past glory and their destiny. 2 vols. (London: Werner Laurie, 1911.)

Friedrich S. Krauss. Südslavische Hexensagen. (Vienna, 1884.)
—— Sitte und Brauch der Südslaven. (Vienna, 1885.)
—— Slavische Volkforschungen. (Leipzig, 1908.)

Edward Gibbon. Decline and Fall of the Roman Empire. (Bury's ed. 1898 (vii.).)

Jovan Tomić. Naučni pregled: Ponovno narodno pevanje. Književni Glasnik. Aug.–Oct. 1907.

Sr J. Stojković. Kraljević Marko, 65 pp. (Belgrade, 1907.)
—— Postanak i Poreklo narodnih pesama o Kraljeviću Marku. (Belgrade, 1921.)

Stanoje Stanojević. Istorija Srpskoga Naroda. (Belgrade, 1908.)
Dr T. Maretić. Naša narodna epika. 263 pp. (Zagreb, 1909.)
W. Miller. The Ottoman Empire. (Cambridge, 1913.)
Maximilian A. Mügge. Serbian Folk-songs, Fairy Tales and Pro-
verbs. (London, 1916.)
H. W. V. Temperley. History of Serbia. (London: Bell, 1917.)
L. F. Waring. Serbia. (Home University Library, 1917.)
C. Jireček. Geschichte der Serben. (Gotha, 1911.)
Dr Milan Ćurčin. Das serbische Volkslied in der deutschen Literatur.
(Leipzig, 1905.)
Prof. Pavle Popović. Jugoslovenska Književnost. (Cambridge, 1918.)
Nevill Forbes. The position of the Slavonic Languages at the present
day. (Clarendon Press, 1910.)
—— Serbian Grammar. (In collaboration with Dragutin Subotić.)
(Clarendon Press, 1918), pp. 22–24.
H. Munro Chadwick. The Heroic Age (Cambridge, 1912), pp. 103–
104; pp. 313–319 (The Battle of Kossovo); pp. 441 ff.
Dr Branko Vodnik. Narodne pjesme hrvatsko-srpske. (Zagreb, 1918.)
Helen Rootham. Kossovo, Heroic Songs of the Serbs. (Oxford:
Blackwell, 1920.)
Quarterly Review, vol. xxxv. pp. 66–86. Translations from the Servian
Minstrelsy: to which are added some Specimens of Anglo-Norman
Romances. 4to. (London, 1826.) The article begins: "Of this
volume a very small edition only has been printed for private
circulation...." The specimens given in the Review are sufficiently
good to make one wish there had been more of them. They are
evidently based on Talvj's German version and although it is
not so stated, Lockhart himself was probably the translator. On
page 28 of his "Servian Popular Poetry," Bowring, referring to
the "Translations," comments acidly: "The tasteful author has
no doubt greatly embellished the original."

The Marko cycle, as a whole, has never been translated into
English, but the following books contain renderings of twelve of the
ballads as given in the second volume of Vuk's collection:
"Servian Popular Poetry," by John Bowring. (London, 1827.)
    1. The Moorish King's Daughter.
    2. Marko and the Turks.
    3. Death of Kralevich Marko. (All in unrhymed decasyllables.)
"Servia and the Servians," by Chedo Mijatovich. (London: Pitman,
1908.)
    1. Oorosh and Marko Kralyevich.
    2. The Royal Prince Marko and the Veela.
    3. Kralyevich Marko and Moossa Kessejiya.
    4. How Marko abolished the wedding-tax. (All in prose.)

"Hero-tales and Legends of the Serbians," by W. M. Petrovitch.
(London: Harrap, 1914.)
1. The Marriage of King Voukashin.
2. Prince Marko tells whose the Empire shall be.
3. Prince Marko and a Moorish Chieftain.
4. Prince Marko abolishes the wedding-tax.
5. Prince Marko and Bogdan the Bully.
6. Prince Marko and General Voutcha.
7. Prince Marko's wedding-procession.
8. Prince Marko and the Moorish Princess.
9. Prince Marko and the Veela.
10. Prince Marko and the Turkish huntsmen.
11. Prince Marko and Moussa Kessedjiya.
12. The Death of Prince Marko. (All in prose.)
"Serbian Songs and Poems: Chords of the Yugoslav Harp," by
J. W. Wiles. (London: George Allen and Unwin, 1917.)
Mostly short lyrical pieces. Contains a metrical rendering of
"Marko and the Falcon."
"Serbian Ballads," by R. W. Seton-Watson, has metrical translation
of "Marko and the Vila" (not Vuk's version). "Serbian
Ballads" is a pamphlet of sixteen pages published by the
Kossovo Day Committee, 1916.

INDEX

For EU product safety concerns, contact us at Calle de José Abascal, 56–1°,
28003 Madrid, Spain or eugpsr@cambridge.org.

www.ingramcontent.com/pod-product-compliance
Ingram Content Group UK Ltd.
Pitfield, Milton Keynes, MK11 3LW, UK
UKHW010042140625
459647UK00012BA/1562